Learning and Teaching

ONE WEEK LOAN

Also available

Professional Values and Practice
The Essential Guide for Higher Level Teaching Assistants
Anne Watkinson
1-84312-250-2

The Essential Guide for Experienced Teaching Assistants
Meeting the National Occupational Standards at Level 3
Anne Watkinson
1-84312-009-7

The Essential Guide for Competent Teaching Assistants
Meeting the National Occupational Standards at Level 2
Anne Watkinson
1-84312-008-9

Assisting Learning and Supporting Teaching
A Practical Guide for the Teaching Assistant in the Classroom
Anne Watkinson
1-85346-794-4

Learning and Teaching

The Essential Guide for Higher Level Teaching Assistants

ANNE WATKINSON

David Fulton Publishers

This edition reprinted 2007 by Routledge
2 Park Square, Milton Park, Abingdon, Oxon, OX14 4RN
Simultaneously published in the USA and Canada
By Routledge
270 Madison Avenue, New York, NY 10016

Reprinted 2006

The right of Anne Watkinson to be identified as the author of this work has been asserted
by her in accordance with the Copyright, Designs and Patents Act 1988.

British Library Cataloguing in Publication Data
A catalogue record for this book is available from the British Library.

ISBN: 1 84312 251 0

10 9 8 7 6 5 4 3 2

Typeset by RefineCatch Limited, Bungay, Suffolk
Printed and bound in the UK by Ashford Colour Press Ltd, Gosport, Hants.

Contents

Preface

This is an exciting time for teaching assistants (TAs). Your role in supporting and promoting the learning and teaching of all children and young people is being accompanied by considerable funding for development and recognition. There are a lot of different levels you can now work at, depending on your own abilities and the needs of your school. The role has been compared with that of nurses working alongside doctors – a complementary addition to the teaching staff of a school.

The recognition of the various levels has brought about a whole host of training programmes for TAs: induction training, National Occupational Standards at levels 2 and 3; and now standards at a higher level have been published by the Teacher Training Agency (TTA) – now the Training and Development Agency for Schools (TDA). This book is aimed at those TAs either who are being appointed at Higher Level Teaching Assistant (HLTA) level or who are working towards HLTA status recognition. HLTAs, by the very nature of the expectations surrounding the role, should be able to read widely, consult and discuss issues with school colleagues.

This book should stimulate thought and action, promote discussion and create opportunities for reflection – key skills for HLTAs. This particular volume aims to deal with the more practical aspects of the teaching and learning part of the HLTA role; a companion volume is also available* which deals with the underlying philosophy and principles of practice. Both books are needed to underpin your HLTA status and to get you thinking about the generic issues of the role, but you will need to read further to cover specific curriculum or special needs aspects.

Professional Values and Practice: The Essential Guide for Higher Level Teaching Assistants by Anne Watkinson, 2005, David Fulton Publishers.

Acknowledgements

I would like to thank:

- the schools, LEA advisers and colleagues with whom I have discussed the many issues that this initiative raises;

- the staff of schools who have been so willing to spend time with me and tell me about their successes and attempts at making sense of the school workforce remodelling intentions and practicalities;

- the staff and pupils of Clacton High School, Colne Community School, Manningtree High School and Alresford Primary School, who have shared their experiences with me and allowed me to observe and photograph their teaching and learning in action;

- Clacton High School and Manningtree High School, who have allowed me to reproduce some of their school's documentation;

- the many schools, TAs and HLTAs whose practice and friendship has been a constant inspiration throughout my work with them, but particularly Dee Weedon and Jenni Mills;

- Margaret Marriott of David Fulton Publishers, for her continuing positive feedback and help while preparing the book. Without her gentle nudging it might not have got written;

- my husband Frank, for his endless patience, domestic help and support with my ICT systems.

Abbreviations

ASE	Association for Science Education
CPD	Continuing professional development
DfES	Department for Education and Skills
EAL	English as an additional language
HLTA	Higher Level Teaching Assistant
HMI	Her Majesty's Inspectorate
ICT	Information and communications technology
IEP	Individual Education Plan
INSET	In-service education for teachers
ITA	Initial teaching alphabet
LEA	Local Education Authority
NC	National Curriculum
NOS	National Occupational Standards
NVQ	National Vocational Qualification
Ofsted	Office for Standards in Education
PANDA	Performance and Assessment
PPA	Planning, preparation and assessment
PRU	Pupil referral unit
QCA	Qualifications and Curriculum Authority
QTS	Qualified Teacher Status
SAT	Standard Assessment Task or Test
SDP	School development plan
SEN	Special educational needs
SENCO	Special Educational Needs Co-ordinator
SIP	School improvement plan
SOW	Scheme of work
TA	Teaching assistant
TTA	Teacher Training Agency
VAK	Visual, auditory and kinaesthetic
ZPD	Zone of Proximal Development

CHAPTER 1

Introduction

Background

This book is the second of a pair written to support the acquisition of the Higher Level Teaching Assistant (HLTA) standards (www.hlta.gov.uk). The introduction of HLTAs is part of the reform of the school workforce set out in a National Agreement on raising standards and tackling teachers' workload made in January 2003 (DfES 2003a). The books cover the generic issues which underpin all that you do as an HLTA, whether specialising in a particular subject or in special educational needs (SEN), at any Key Stage.

The first book dealt with the set of standards about the values and principles which underpin the practice of learning and teaching. They will hold whatever the subject matter, or whoever is being taught or is teaching. This second one covers the putting of those principles into practice, again in a generic way whatever the age group or the particular needs of pupils with whom you are working. The books are not courses in themselves, nor do they pretend to provide the last word in the area. Whatever stage you are at in your career path as a teaching assistant (TA), you have continuing professional development (CPD) needs. Reading and reflection are part of this process. You need to meet, exchange views and see examples of good practice, find out about the latest resources and keep abreast of new ideas in education, teaching and learning and about children and young people themselves. Above all, you need to be working in a school, preferably where all the staff take part in in-service education for teachers (INSET) activities, where you will feel able to ask questions and find support of various kinds.

These HLTA books will not provide the detailed information you need for curriculum subject knowledge and understanding, nor are they intended to help you with understanding the specific SEN of individual pupils. They do not, therefore, cover all the standards. Standards 2.1, 2.2, 2.3, 2.4, 2.6 and 2.8 will all require more detailed study than either of these books will provide. To gain HLTA status you have to show that you fulfil *all* of the standards. They are to be seen as a holistic set, not a set from which you can pick and choose as with the National Vocational Qualifications (NVQs). Also, you should remember that HLTA status, if awarded, is not a qualification; it is a recognition of your competence and ability to do the job.

The previous three books in the TA series were to help TAs develop their thoughts at various stages before the higher level. One of the books, *Assisting Learning and Supporting*

Teaching, was written to give some background after the introduction of the induction training materials (Watkinson 2002). The other two were written to support those TAs undertaking qualifications or wanting background reading when working at levels 2 and 3 of the National Occupational Standards (NOS). These were called *The Essential Guide for Competent Teaching Assistants* and *The Essential Guide for Experienced Teaching Assistants* (Watkinson 2003a; 2003b). They contain useful materials for those of you considering HLTA status without going through each of the earlier levels, particularly about finding your way round a school, the education system and developing your own skills, and will be referred to on occasions in this book.

Hopefully, if you are participating in any formal course or assessment briefing for HLTA status, you will have a mentor. It is important for an HLTA that this be a teaching staff member, as you will need to learn about and watch many of the activities of the teachers; you will be teaching classes, not acting as a cover supervisor. If you go for HLTA assessment, you will need a spokesperson teacher to talk with the assessor. It is possible that a more senior TA could be a suitable mentor for the lower levels of TA. No book or course can provide you with all you need to work as an HLTA; actual practice in schools must be both observed and experienced by you alongside discussion with relevant staff about what and how things are done. All schools are different; they have their own policies and procedures, both written and understood.

The structure of the book

The prevailing philosophy at the time of writing is that, given what to teach and how and when to teach, the pupils will learn and achieve certain levels of attainment appropriate to their age. Given the emphasis over the last 30 years on helping those with SEN achieve their potential, there is clear recognition that some children will take longer or need special help in order to achieve the age-related 'norms'. This centrally directed strategy has introduced a much-needed structure into many schools, which has resulted in some excellent teaching materials, and has challenged poor expectations. However, it has stifled creativity and imagination, restricted teachers from using their imagination and provided a 'one system fits all' approach. This has resulted in pupils being unable to generalise the skills learnt and a lack of opportunity for pupils to achieve in more artistic or physical avenues. It is tempting for an aspiring HLTA to assume that all he or she has to do is understand and practise the appropriate bit of the curriculum or national strategy and 'deliver' it. This book will not help you succeed via that route. All of us are learners; we were when younger and we will continue learning into old age, if only how to cope with having to wear glasses or sneak a nap after lunch! We all have differing learning needs and styles, but understanding these is not sufficient for us to learn; we also need appropriate instruction. Teaching and learning have to go together in order to maximise the time spent in school. This book is to help you make sense of that combination, so that with the materials you can access in school you will become an understanding, reflective and successful practitioner, not just an automaton.

Chapter 2 sets the scene discussing the relationship of teaching to learning, setting it in the current climate. Chapter 3 will look more closely at the current theories of how we learn, a complex and intriguing field which is developing fast with new medical technology. However, learning is not a straightforward and linear physical or psychological process, so Chapter 4 looks more closely at factors that can influence it. Chapter 5, recognising the complexity of the learning process, gives some general strategies that can be employed by teachers and HLTAs to support different learning styles and needs. This book, however, will not cover the specific learning needs of individual children with SEN or whose English is an additional language (EAL). However well a teacher or HLTA understands all this theory, when it comes to the interface between adult and pupils the context in which you work will alter the situation. You have to take account of the requirements of the curriculum for your school and the kinds of pupils with whom you will be working. Chapter 6 looks at ways of considering the curriculum to maximise learning and strategies of behaviour management. Chapters 7, 8 and 9 will take you through the process of teaching from the identification of what is to be taught, planning and preparation, and the kind of face-to-face strategies that are of use in the classroom with pupils, to the ways in which you can assess what has been taught and then tell others, including the pupils themselves, about it. Chapter 10 brings the whole book to a conclusion.

As with the level 2 and level 3 NOS, many of the HLTA standards need to be cross-referenced; for instance, professional values and practice must hold through all the teaching and learning activities or they are pointless. Factors like relationships, which underpin all of teaching and learning, were dealt with in the first book (Watkinson 2005). Thus they will only be mentioned in passing but their crucial role must be kept in mind at all times. In trying to link learning and teaching so closely together, I have a more holistic and apparently mixed approach than the standards can indicate. By their nature they have to be a list. Table 1.1, below, gives you a rough guide as to where to find individual standards as they are referred to in this book.

Using the book

It is possible to read the book straight through, but hopefully you will be reading passages between work sessions and possibly even course sessions. You will therefore be able to relate the text to your own experience. As you are aiming to be a thinking, reflective practitioner, you also need to read more widely than this book. Each chapter will give some recommended reading for you to dip into. Some of the books referred to may seem rather theoretical and possibly difficult to read, but you are now expected to be working at second year degree level equivalent for the HLTA status. You should be able to dip into the books and seek out relevant passages or chapters fairly easily and hopefully will have a good grasp of most of the educational jargon. To follow the references to the standards made in this book – either direct references or the numbers in square brackets – you will need both a copy of the standards (DfES and TTA 2003) and the most recent copy of the TTA *Guidance to the Standards* (TTA 2005).

There are some examples of practice given in the book, but you should be able to add some of your own. If you are undertaking any kind of study for accreditation you will have to write assignments or accounts of your practice to exemplify your understanding of the

Table 1.1   The general areas of this text relating to the HLTA standards

Chapter	Main thrust of chapter	Some related standards to consider
1 Introduction		1.6
2 Teaching and learning	3.3.1	1.2, 1.4 2.5
3 Learning development	2.5	2.8
4 Influences on learning	2.5	1.2, 1.5
5 Strategies to support learning	2.3, 2.9 3.3.1	1.2 2.5
6 Context of learning: the curriculum and pupil behaviour	2.9 3.3.4	1.1, 1.2, 1.3 2.1, 2.2, 2.3, 2.8
7 Planning and preparation	3.1	1.1, 1.4 2.3, 2.4 3.3.8
8 Performance	3.3	1.1, 1.2, 1.3 2.4, 2.9
9 Assessment, monitoring, feedback and recording	3.2	1.1, 1.4, 1.5, 2.3, 2.5
10 In conclusion		1.4, 1.6

standards. I suggest you keep a diary notebook; not a day-by-day diary, just an exercise book or looseleaf pad with a ring binder to keep the notes in. Make notes of events or lessons that went particularly well, or interactions with pupils, or things that went wrong and how you would do them differently. Always date such accounts. These need not be long, just a couple of paragraphs. Then, when you come to write up your tasks or assignments you will have a source of material on which to draw, and you can then relate the event to a standard as indicated by your tutor. Always remember that when writing such accounts you are writing about other people or other people's children, so you should keep such notes safely, and if you use them in any essay or report you must change the names to anonymise the account.

Finally, there are some reflective activities that you can undertake or discuss with a colleague. The intention is that you use the book actively, not passively.

Essential reading

DfES and TTA (2003) *Professional Standards for Higher Level Teaching Assistants*. London: Department for Education and Skills and Teacher Training Agency.

TTA (2005) *Guidance to the Standards: Meeting the Professional Standards for the Award of Higher Level Teaching Assistants*. London: Teacher Training Agency.

Some further reading

Watkinson, A. (2003b) *The Essential Guide for Experienced Teaching Assistants: Meeting the National Occupational Standards at Level 3*. London: David Fulton Publishers.

Watkinson, A. (2005) *Professional Values and Practice: The Essential Guide for Higher Level Teaching Assistants*. London: David Fulton Publishers.

Useful websites

www.hlta.gov.uk
www.tta.gov.uk/hlta

CHAPTER 2

Teaching and learning

Defining teaching

Teaching should be seen as enabling learning. The word itself has caused problems, particularly in relation to the establishment of HLTAs. Some teachers, that is those with Qualified Teacher Status (QTS), are concerned that by allowing HLTAs to teach, and teach whole classes as well, it is undermining the hard work they had to undertake in order to obtain their QTS. They feel that only those with QTS can and should teach. Suggestions that teachers might be able to take groups of 60 pupils or more have not helped. These ideas are considered by some to be detrimental to pupils' learning and causing possible teacher redundancies, yet they have not recognised that talks, plays, assemblies, film shows and informal times already regularly take place with only a few people present who have QTS.

Also, we all teach each other: parents teach their children, children teach each other. I have watched TAs, formally and informally, in nearly 300 schools, and it is obvious that TAs are teaching, even though they do not have all the attributes of a qualified teacher. As a TA or HLTA you must still act under the direction of qualified teachers at all times, and these teachers take responsibility for the learning of the pupils in their class, including anything you do. This responsibility covers:

(a) planning and preparing lessons and courses for pupils;
(b) delivering lessons for pupils;
(c) assessing the development, progress and attainment of pupils;
(d) reporting on the development, progress and attainment of pupils; and
(e) marking the work of pupils.

(DfES 2003b: 7)

The recognition of the proper use of teachers and TAs, HLTAs and other support staff is possibly the most important or difficult challenge facing schools in the immediate future. The premise is that qualified teachers are too precious a resource to spend on doing tasks which other people can do as well if not better. Also, the principle is maintained that teachers, including head teachers, should have a workload that matches their job description. Talents and qualifications other than QTS should be recognised and utilised to their best purpose.

You can try your dictionary or a thesaurus to clarify the meaning of words. Most dictionary definitions of teaching can be applied to the work of TAs, but they could also be used about many other categories of people interacting with children. We need to look at educational definitions. Ask your TA and teacher colleagues, 'what do you mean by teaching?'; they may use the word *pedagogy*, the art or study of teaching. The definition I like best is that pedagogy or teaching is 'any conscious activity by one person designed to enhance the learning in another' (Watkins and Mortimore 1999: 3). This again is a general definition which could fit many people, and is not necessarily associated with schools.

One definition that some teachers will come up with is that used by the Office for Standards in Education (Ofsted) inspectors. Indeed, a TA or HLTA taking a class will, in the new inspections, be observed by inspectors, and the definitions found in the guidance for teachers will be used by inspectors to evaluate the TA's work, but Ofsted does not have the only definition of 'teaching' or 'teachers'. Another definition can be found by looking at the QTS published standards (TTA 2002), and you will find there is considerable resemblance between the QTS standards and the HLTA standards. In fact, the QTS standards provided a model, both sets being produced by the Teacher Training Agency (TTA), and the similarities are deliberate. While they are similar, the differences make it clear there is much more to being a qualified teacher than meets the eye.

Find a copy of the guidance for Ofsted inspectors

Find the pages in the handbook about teaching
You will find the section begins with what the inspectors must evaluate and report on, followed by a list of things for inspectors to consider. To know how inspectors decide whether teaching and learning is good or not, look at where this is described (page 62 in the primary and nursery schools handbook (Ofsted 2003)). These judgements would be the same for teachers or assistants working in a teaching role. (For example, your deployment, effectiveness, guidance and training are also considered in an inspection, see page 68.) This is followed first by a description of what the inspection should focus on and how the inspector should form judgements. These are then followed by a whole lot of questions, printed in bold, which the inspectors should or could use. Each question is followed by statements and descriptions of why this is important and what kinds of things inspectors will see. There are then grids with descriptors of what constitutes Excellent (1) through to Very Poor (7) practice.

Find a copy of the QTS standards (on the TTA website)
Compare this with the HLTA standards. Note the differences and discuss them with your mentor. Decide whether the differences are just in phrasing or are fundamental to your role and that of the teacher. Note in the QTS standards particularly:

1.8
the detail of 2.1
the careful wording of 3.1.1–3.1.4
the detail of 3.2 and 3.3.

Can you and your mentor recognise how much more the teacher with QTS has to know, understand and take responsibility for?

TAs do teach, but do not take the responsibility for the direction and organisation of the learning. Remember that the classroom teacher must take the lead in setting out the objectives of the lessons and the strategies by which these can be achieved, provide the role model and direct the activities [3.1.2]. The whole process is carefully regulated for HLTAs as part of the 2002 Education Act (DfES 2003b). You will still have to agree your boundaries with any teacher you work with in order to make sure you have dealt with any sensitivities that may exist about your status and role in their class.

The teaching process

Being a good teacher is not about being able to tick a list of skills, although skills are needed and can be taught and practised, nor is it a question of being an expert in a subject. Sometimes, those who are highly qualified academically in a subject do not make good teachers. Some relatively uneducated people with no skills training can be the best teachers in some areas, for instance helping a baby in their first steps. There is an element of personality which is able to communicate, to listen and watch for reactions, to relate to their audience whether adult or child about the subject in question. Relationships between the learner and the teacher are important. There can be elements of artistry in teaching.

Models of teaching have been proposed at various times. The Literacy Hour, for example, is only one approach with various models contained therein: didactic introduction, group work and plenary. Investigative, practical work or repetitive drill for rote learning are others. A good teacher understands that all the aspects – skills, personality, knowledge of content and different delivery methods – are needed. Sadly, the model of teaching that the Hay/McBer consultancy used (see Figure 2.1) when they investigated teacher effectiveness

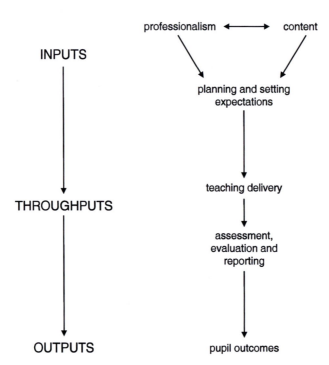

Figure 2.1   The input/output model from Hay/McBer's *Mapping the National Standards* of various professional grades of teacher

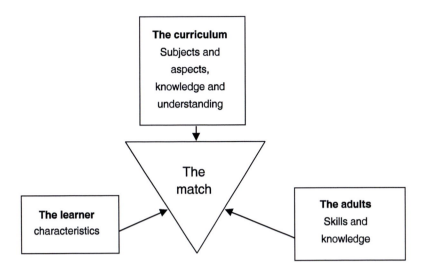

Figure 2.2 The match between the curriculum, the learner and the adults in the classroom (Watkinson 2002: 11)

and tried to decide what makes a good teacher ignored the needs, strengths and reactions of pupils (see Figure 2.1). It was a purely outcome model, seeing the teacher as the source of input and the pupil as producing outcomes (Hay/McBer 2000: Appendix 5).

It is generally agreed that all teachers need a combination of styles or approaches to tackle the variety of subjects they teach. However, what goes on in the classroom for the pupil learner depends on the match between what the teacher wants him or her to learn (the curriculum, the learning style and characteristics of the pupil) and the activities of the adults teaching and supporting the learning. The task or activity the learner is asked to do depends for its success on an appropriate match (see Figure 2.2).

If any one of these is inappropriate, then something goes wrong. The curriculum can be too hard or too easy, learners can be unhappy or uncomfortable, or adults may not know what they are talking about or understand what they are supposed to be doing. Standards 3.1.2, 3.1.3 and 3.2.2 all indicate the situation regarding the pupils must be taken into account.

Principles of learning and teaching

During the last few years there has been a plethora of initiatives and new legal frameworks in education. The intention has always been to raise standards, build on existing good practice and eliminate sloppy or poor practice. However, dealing with problem areas, ensuring access to a National Curriculum (NC) while enabling local schools to manage their own affairs, beefing up the inspection system and providing advice and resources have in many cases succeeded in straitjacketing teaching and learning. The overall impression is that central directives are trying to make one pattern fit all kinds of school and all sorts of learner. In fact, this is not the case. The NC is a minimum entitlement, schools do have their own budgets and considerable autonomy, inspections cause more fear than is intended, and strategies have been followed to the letter instead of adopted appropriately for a situation.

The recent Primary Strategy is an attempt to explore these ideas and rectify some of the misunderstandings. Its very name *Excellence and Enjoyment* (DfES 2003c) shows the concern over the limitations on educational experience that previous initiatives have produced. You should be able to find this document easily if you are in a primary school, and I recommend, even if you are not, that you have a look at it. You can download it or talk to someone from your local primary school to borrow a copy. To support this document there is also a large plastic box with INSET resources so that schools can look at the implications of the document for their practice. Several of the booklets from this pack will be referred to as I go through this book. The box also contains videos and CDs of examples of good practice in action and extra readings. Ask whether your school has been using this material in their staff meetings, and find out how it has helped and what has been particularly useful.

In this original document, some useful principles of learning and teaching are spelt out. The order of the words in that sentence and in the title of this book is also significant. 'Learning' is put before 'teaching' rather than the more usual phrase 'teaching and learning'. There is a recognition that the purpose of teaching is learning. For some, the emphasis on learning in these materials loses sight of the importance of the instructional side of teaching, and heralds a return to 'learning by discovery' which failed so many pupils. They must be seen in relation to and as a reaction to the current circumstances where 'delivery of the curriculum' has been the watchword of teaching. Good schools and good teachers have always maintained a balance between teacher direction and enabling, and responded to the needs of their pupils and the subject matter being covered. The role of the teacher, in having appropriate skills for different situations, being themselves sufficiently well informed, being sensitive to the various needs of learners and being responsible for the progress of the learners in their care, is still paramount.

The document defines the following principles which, although in a publication for primary schools, are generic whatever the age of pupil or phase of school.

> Good learning and teaching should:
> - **Ensure every child succeeds:** provide an inclusive education within a culture of high expectations.
> - **Build on what learners already know:** structure and pace teaching so that students know what is to be learnt, how and why.
> - **Make learning vivid and real:** develop understanding through enquiry, creativity, e-learning and group problem solving.
> - **Make learning an enjoyable and challenging experience:** stimulate learning through matching teaching techniques and strategies to a range of learning styles.
> - **Enrich the learning experience:** build learning skills across the curriculum.
> - **Promote assessment for learning:** make children partners in their learning.
>
> (DfES 2003c: 29)

Facilitating learning

A good teacher is always aware of the learning needs of his or her class, and adapts the teaching programme to match those needs. These needs may reflect the ways in which the pupils learn [2.5], or adjusting to physical, emotional, social, cultural or spiritual differences [3.1.3]. Some of the ways in which we adapt what we do are instinctive, because of our personality; some people are more able than others to empathise with other people. This may be due to experience, having brought up a family, or having worked with learners, both children and adults, and noticed what does or does not help. When you start as a TA, the tendency is to operate merely as a 'keeper' or 'task minder', ensuring the pupils keep their 'nose to the grindstone'. Your role can be so much more than that, and as an HLTA it should be.

MacGilchrist *et al.* (1997; 2004) write about teaching for learning. They say there are two main features that contribute to success: 'The first is an approach that emphasizes reflection and interaction about the learning taking place as well as instruction.

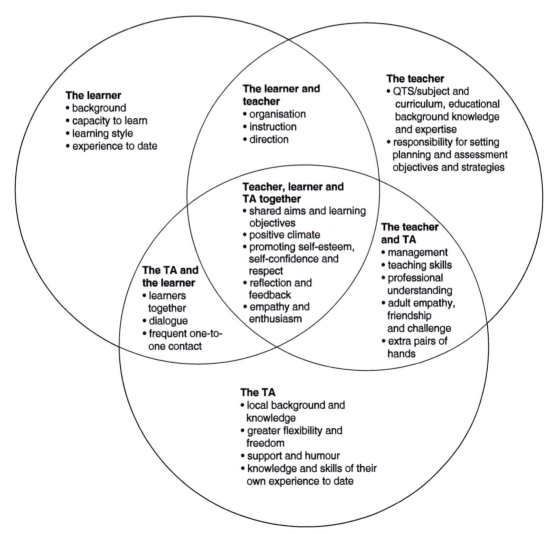

Figure 2.3   The interactions of teachers, TAs and pupils in the classroom
(from Watkinson 2002: 51)

The second is respect for the learners and their learning processes in a way which enables everyone in the classroom to be involved.' (MacGilchrist *et al.* 2004: 87). They argue that 'teaching is a complex and sophisticated craft when it is done well. It is composed of distinct but interrelated parts and cannot be separated from its interrelationship with learning.' I took their learning pact diagram showing what teacher and learner both need to bring to a learning situation and reinterpreted it for TAs. If you add a TA to the classroom the dynamics change (see Figure 2.3).

You may well be on your own with pupils, either individually, or in a group, or now, as an aspiring HLTA, for a whole class. You will bring much-enhanced skills, knowledge and understanding from when you were that trainee TA envisaged in my first book (Watkinson 2002), and you will still need to make your own pact with the learners as a teacher would, building your relationships with the teachers you will be working. You will need to ensure that pupils understand that you work with the class teacher; he/she will be monitoring the outcomes, but you have a role in your own right (see Figure 2.4).

It is worth taking time with the teacher you work most closely with to explore what his or her expectations of your work are, and how will enable you to perform to your best. You should make explicit things that may otherwise be implicit [1.1]. When such things are not discussed, misunderstandings can arise and it can take much longer to establish how you work together.

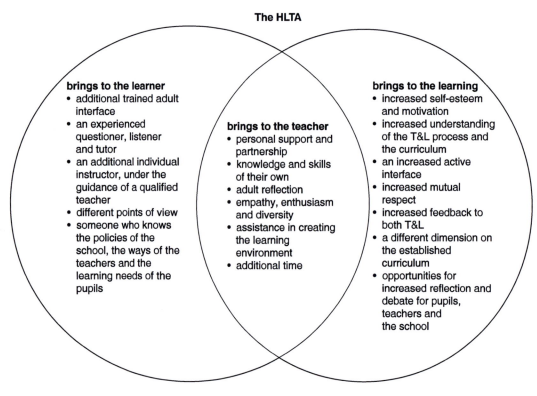

The HLTA

brings to the learner
- additional trained adult interface
- an experienced questioner, listener and tutor
- an additional individual instructor, under the guidance of a qualified teacher
- different points of view
- someone who knows the policies of the school, the ways of the teachers and the learning needs of the pupils

brings to the teacher
- personal support and partnership
- knowledge and skills of their own
- adult reflection
- empathy, enthusiasm and diversity
- assistance in creating the learning environment
- additional time

brings to the learning
- increased self-esteem and motivation
- increased understanding of the T&L process and the curriculum
- an increased active interface
- increased mutual respect
- increased feedback to both T&L
- a different dimension on the established curriculum
- opportunities for increased reflection and debate for pupils, teachers and the school

Figure 2.4   The teaching and learning role of the HLTA

Establishing boundaries
You could use the diagram above and talk it through with your mentor or teacher.
Before you work for a different teacher find out (if you do not know already):

what the system of planning is for that year or subject;
when you can talk things over with the teacher before and after the lesson(s)/session(s) you are to take;
where you can find materials to work with;
what reading or research you need to do before the lesson;
whether you can approach the teacher during the lesson;
what decisions you can make for yourself;
which pupils you are going to work with and their particular needs;
what the learning intentions are of the teacher whose session you will be undertaking;
what kind of end product the teacher expects (or is it the doing of the task that is important, or both);
what to do if the pupils misbehave or things go wrong and you cannot cope;
whether there are any specific health and safety issues for the area in which you will be working;
what to do if pupils finish what the teacher intended;
whether you are to set homework;
whether you will be able to follow up anything;
whether you are to mark any books; and
how you can tell the teacher how the pupils did the task.

Establish some lines of communication for the future to ensure:

you understand the needs of the pupils with whom you are to work;
how you can best prepare or follow up work;
how to find out what the teacher wants you to do on a regular basis, and what the pupils are expected to learn and achieve in the time you are with them;
what sorts of things you can do or plan to do on your own initiative.

You may well have already decided what your style is; which teachers of those you have seen you admire, and which teachers, when you were at school, had the most effect upon you. You may feel you cannot change how you will behave in front of a class. This is not the case. You do need to think deeply about your purpose in being with a class and realise that your current experience may be limited, however large your school.

Extending your experience
Ask to watch different teachers in action from those you know well.
What kind of subject matter or activities interest the pupils?
What strategies do the teachers use to get the pupils quiet when they want to address the class?
Does the pupil seating arrangement affect the attention mode of the pupils?
Are there organisational strategies which help or hinder the learning process?

Ask to visit other schools, to watch, listen and learn.
Discuss strategies and activities with your mentor, remembering to be tactful when discussing colleagues' methods.
If you have access to a library try one or two of the chapters listed below and think about the nature of this job called teaching.

As your class and group sizes increase so does your responsibility for the learning of those pupils. Hopefully, the subsequent chapters will also give you food for thought and help as you develop.

Essential reading

DfES and TTA (2003) *Professional Standards for Higher Level Teaching Assistants*. London: Department for Education and Skills and Teacher Training Agency.

TTA (2005) *Guidance to the Standards: Meeting the Professional Standards for the Award of Higher Level Teaching Assistant*. London: Teacher Training Agency.

Some further reading

The art and skill of teaching

Brooks, V. (2004) 'Learning to teach and learning about teaching', in V. Brooks, I. Abbott and L. Bills (eds) *Preparing to Teach in Secondary Schools*. Maidenhead and New York: Open University Press and McGraw-Hill Education, pp. 7–17.

'The principles and practice of good teaching', in D. Hayes, (2000) *The Handbook for Newly Qualified Teachers: Meeting the Standards in Primary and Middle Schools*. London: David Fulton Publishers, pp. 20–37.

'Teaching for learning', in B. MacGilchrist, K. Myers, and J. Reed, (2004) *The Intelligent School* (2nd edn). London; Thousand Oaks, CA and New Delhi: Sage, pp. 71–91.

McIntyre, D. (2000) 'The nature of classroom teaching expertise', D. Whitebread (ed.) *The Psychology of Teaching and Learning in the Primary School*. London and New York: RoutledgeFalmer, pp. 1–14.

If you want a more technical book, try dipping into Mortimore, P. (ed.) (1999) *Understanding Pedagogy and Its Impact on Learning*. London; Thousand Oaks, CA and New Delhi: Paul Chapman, Sage Publications (Inc.) and Sage Publications India Pvt Ltd.

Useful websites

www.fultonpublishers.co.uk
www.lg-employers.gov.uk
www.remodelling.org
www.teachernet.gov.uk/teachingassistants
www.tta.gov.uk/hlta

CHAPTER 3

Learning development

All animals learn. It is one of the characteristics of living things that they change as they grow and respond to their environments. Human beings are designed to learn all their life; they depend on it in ways that apply less to other animals. Even other mammals have many more instinctive or inbuilt behaviour patterns than we do. It is almost impossible to observe learning taking place; what we see is the behaviour or performance changes which result from learning. Recent developments in brain scanning are producing interesting observations of the changes taking place in the brain during learning, but even here the significance is only to be guessed at. This chapter is a very simplified version of the theories to date, but it may spur you on to find out more for yourself [1.6, 2.7]. Some of the content of this and following chapters is an expanded version of material from my previous books.

If you are new to considering learning on its own, or think it is straightforward, try the following exercise. If you can do it with a group of friends, you will begin to see not only where the complexities are, but also that quite different learning experiences have similarities in the process.

How do you learn?
Recall a recent learning experience. It can be a formal one such as a course or evening class; a life experience such as coping with family changes, bringing up children, even divorce or bereavement; using a new piece of equipment like a new video (or DVD) recorder; or learning to drive. The context does not matter, but you need to remember it fairly clearly.

Just jot down a few things about that experience, describing it briefly
What made you undertake it? Why did you do it? Was it necessity or whim?
What or who helped you start?
What or who helped you during the process?
What or who hindered during the process?
Was it the same all the way through? If not how did it vary?
What else would have helped or could have been done to help you?
What feelings did you have during the process?

> What skills and knowledge did you acquire?
> Did anything you did or learnt relate to anything else in your life?
> Have you finished? If not, will it finish?
> What would you change now with hindsight?
>
> (Watkinson 2002: 27)

In doing this with different groups of people I have found the following:

- Learning is not a straightforward process. It has ups and downs, and even goes backwards at times.
- Time and timing is important.
- Learning rarely finishes, even in a restricted area, even if the course itself does. We go on learning all our lives.
- People can help and hinder. Another person who has more experience of the same area can be helpful – this may be a teacher or a course tutor but does not have to be.
- Information and communications technology (ICT) alone and distance learning packages have their place, but discussion with fellow learners supports the process.
- Previous life experiences always help somewhere.
- Correct tools or words or strategies usually help.
- Challenge and motivation are significant factors.
- Most learners experience fear and anxiety as well as satisfaction.
- Attitudes to learning are important.

Learning is influenced by the inherited characteristics of the learner and his or her developmental rate, both influenced by environmental factors. These can be serendipitous factors or those designed to support learning. Abstract learning or thinking or reasoning is only one part of the learning process, although one which teachers (in the widest sense) generally concentrate on. Even learning to eat and drink, without which we would not survive, is subject to internal and external influences. In schools, learning is not just about referring to accumulating skills or factual knowledge, but to developing understanding. It is increasingly recognised that the learning of attitudes and our emotional state, what is sometimes referred to as the affective domain of learning, are also important. We all learn in different ways, as well as having distinct inherited characteristics, and living in unique environments.

Despite these differences, the similarities enable us to teach children or people in groups, while making allowances for the differences. It is generally recognised that by the age of 10 or 11, the age at which most of our children change from a primary to a secondary school, the spread of intellectual ability is at least 7 years. This does not make any allowance for children with profound difficulties or for budding geniuses. This gap will increase, not decrease, as the children get older. We still teach young people in schools in year groups, expecting most to conform to some median position sufficiently to make year-based planning feasible. Selecting children by ability, in separate schools or by streaming or setting, seems an obvious way round this problem, yet it tends to reinforce differences, not support them. The trouble is that ability which is testable in one area may not reflect learning potential in another area, or recognise all the other factors which affect that learning. The social groupings around age-related factors seems to be the best option. Our schools are thus generally organised in age groupings, recognising friendships where possible, with built-in options to specialise and support.

Consider the class groupings in your school
Look at the age distribution of the pupils – is there the same number in each year group? If so why, and how does this come about? There must be some kind of selection criteria, as unequal numbers of children will have been born in a particular area over the years.
Discuss with your mentor why groupings are as they are.
It may be tradition for that school; for example, the rooms were built for two classes for each year group, often called a two-form entry.
It may be a small school with only three teachers for 6 or 7 year groups. Why? How are the schemes of work arranged?
What formal setting or streaming goes on in the school?
What grouping arrangements are made in various classes? Why?
Does it help results? Does it help the teachers? Does it help the pupils? Has anybody checked?
Ask them what they feel about the systems in place in your school, and whether they would like any changes.

Defining learning

One problem, touched on above, is that different people and pupils will have different ideas of what is meant by learning. 'Have the pupils in your group/class/school learnt anything?' This question may well be asked of you as you go forward as an HLTA. One of the distinguishing marks of an HLTA as distinct from a cover supervisor is that the pupils in your care should be making progress because of your action, not just the planning of the teacher. Can what is learnt be measured even if the process itself is difficult to track?

Consider your learning situation again
Did you learn all that you or the teacher intended?
How do you know?
What else did you learn along the way?
Be honest – what about:

how to get to a venue by a quicker route?
how to purchase the tools you needed – including pencils – more cheaply?
considering never to do such a thing again?
what to do when sitting next to someone you disliked?
how to act confidently when you didn't feel it?
making sure the reason for not learning doesn't happen again?

> Did you make any new friends?
> If you passed a test or exam at the end of the process did it test all the things you learnt?
> Why not? Should it have? Could it?
> What do you remember now? What can you do now that you could not do before? Has it
> changed your views on anything or anybody?
> What can you do to recall what you learnt?

Interestingly, when it comes to actually defining learning, most books on the subject assume we all know what it is and do not define it; most dictionaries refer only to acquiring knowledge or committing things to memory. One definition of learning I have used in the past is: 'Learning ... that reflective activity which enables the learner to draw upon previous experience, to understand and evaluate the present, so as to shape future action and formulate new knowledge' (Abbott 1996:1). Ofsted tried to define good and less than satisfactory learning in terms of observable behaviour:

> Where learning is good, most pupils respond readily to the challenge of the
> tasks set, show a willingness to concentrate on them, and make good
> progress. They adjust well to the demands of working in different contexts,
> selecting appropriate methods and organising effectively the resources they
> need. Work is sustained with a sense of commitment and enjoyment. Pupils
> are sufficiently confident and alert to raise questions and to persevere with
> their work when answers are not readily available. They evaluate their own
> work and come to realistic judgements about it. Where appropriate, pupils
> readily help one another.
>
> Where learning is unsatisfactory, pupils are either insufficiently engaged
> in their work, or demonstrate undue dependence on the teacher or uncritical
> use of resources. They are reluctant to take initiatives or accept responsibility.
> They find it difficult to sustain concentration for more than short periods of
> time. They are unable to apply their learning in new contexts.
>
> (Ofsted 1993: 9)

This definition was dropped in the 1995 handbook and replaced by definitions of pupils' responses, attainment and progress. The latest handbooks concentrate on standards and attainment, referring to pupils' learning within the section on teaching. Ofsted recognised that learning itself cannot be seen, only the behaviour which shows itself during and after it has taken place, apart from the heart-stopping moments of seeing 'the penny drop'.

Senge, an expert on industrial management, finding such an interest in his ideas about learning organisations from educationalists, turned his attention to schools. His definition of learning is that it is 'nature's expression of the search for development. It can be diverted or blocked but it can't be prevented from occurring. The core educational task in our time is to evolve the institutions and the practices that assist, not replace that natural learning process.' (Senge *et al.* 2000: 57).

There is sometimes an assumption that learning is a single entity, definable, measurable and irreversible. The sayings 'Learning is about filling empty vessels' or 'teachers delivering the curriculum' come from this source. The input/output model talks of learning outcomes, as though they were some kind of product. One of the readings from Primary National Strategy CD *Intuitive and deliberate learning* has a list of a whole range of outcomes.

> Some varied outcomes of learning:
> - Physical adaptations and habituation
> - Perceptual learning
> - Imitated sequences of actions
> - Learned sequences of skilled movements
> - Changes in attitudes or values
> - Discovering a new strategy
> - Understanding of concepts
> - Remembering of facts
> - Learning of a rule
> - Increased conscious awareness of our own thinking, learning, etc.
>
> (DfES 2004a: 1)

The author goes on to discuss the links between thinking and learning. They are not the same. Learning can be anywhere on a continuum from an unconscious act, through conscious learning, to sitting down and deliberately organising one's reasoning. It can use trial and error methods, reliance on experience alone through problem solving, and following others as in an apprenticeship approach to the kind of academic disciplines practised in universities. The learning can induce habits, require facts to be memorised or involve learning about learning itself.

If we follow this line of reasoning, it means we should try to understand as much about the natural processes as possible, complicated as they are. The measurable outcomes of learning, the products, the matter that can be tested, can be referred to as attainment, not learning itself. This chapter is about the 'how', rather than the 'what'. The process/product argument is a perennial one among educationalists, the reality being that you cannot have one without the other (see Figure 3.1).

In this chapter, while we are concerned with process, you must realise that without the subject matter – knowledge, skills, attitudes and concepts – there would be nothing for the process to work on. Later chapters and other books will refer you to the 'material' or 'subjects' that are learnt.

The learning process

In order to make your planning most effective and provide for the many differences in learning capability and style, you should try to understand as much as you can about what are called 'norms'. These are the stages that researchers, medical practitioners and teachers have identified over the years as the average ages in which children are able to do different

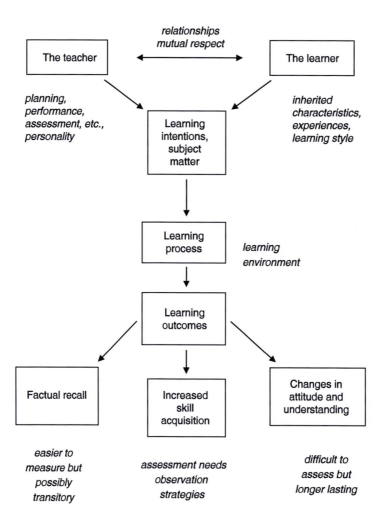

Figure 3.1   The process/product pathways in a school

things. Learning is from conception to death and the adult processes mirror those of childhood. When tackling a new area of learning we 'play around' with the subject, just like a small child. Also, while it is possible just to consider intellectual, or cognitive or reasoning/knowing development separately, it is clear from the simple exercises above that physical, emotional, social, cultural and spiritual factors are often involved. If these facets get out of balance, and one develops but another does not, then the pupil, or adult, can become frustrated, even disturbed. This can be seen sometimes in very bright children whose emotional age matches their chronological age but who may be socially immature and prone to disruptive behaviour. Social or emotional upsets out of school clearly affect pupils' capacity to learn in school.

At the beginning of the chapter you looked at yourself as a learner; hopefully, you have been able to, or will, make opportunities to watch other learners. You must do this with the full knowledge and co-operation of a class teacher and follow the recommended protocols.

Possible protocols to consider for classroom observation
The following needs to be discussed between the TA and the class teacher where any observation is to take place:

- The purpose of the exercise is to . . . e.g. understand more about . . .
- The adults involved will be . . .
- The pupils involved will be . . .

The head teacher/department head/line manager has been told what is happening, and has agreed.
It needs to be checked that:

- anything written was to be shared first with each other so that comments can be made and points of accuracy checked
- any comments to be seen by others will be anonymised, or amalgamated with others to preserve confidentiality
- the main audience of any summary written material would be . . . e.g. the other member of a course, or an outside reader
- the people observed or interviewed can have a copy of the notes made if they so wish
- you know what will happen to any written records
- the intended outcome of the activity is . . .
- you know what you will do if the observation shows up anything within the classroom or school that someone wishes to address or celebrate
- if others get involved, they would be covered by the same sort of protocols
- someone seeks permission of the parents of the children closely involved

Either side should be able to comment at any time during the process if there is any discomfort or suggestion about what is taking place or being said.

(Watkinson 2002: 39, 40)

I also suggested in a previous book that a useful place to start considering the norms of physical development is your family photo album.

Looking at physical norms
Get out your family albums with photographs of either yourself, your family or your children. If you have them, find your children's 'baby books'. Ask other members of your family for some remembrances. Can you identify at what age the following happened? (Try following the development of one child at a time). When did they:

- Sit up on their own
- Turn over
- Crawl
- Stand up unaided
- Walk unaided
- Kick a ball
- Ride a bicycle

- Hold a pencil
- Draw a shape
- Draw a recognisable person
- Write their name
- Catch a ball with one hand
- Skip with a skipping rope
- Tie their own shoelaces?

As you do this with several family members you will begin to see a pattern emerging. Did the boys develop later than the girls in any of these respects?

(Watkinson 2003b: 55)

Genetic and environmental factors

There has long been a debate as to the source of differences from the norms. One of the reasons suggested is the inherited characteristics of each individual. Our characteristics are dependent on our genes; the unique DNA in each of us provides the code for cell development and distribution. However, even in identical twins, who have developed from one fertilised cell splitting, therefore having the same DNA, there are important and distinctive differences. Immediately that first cell splits into two, each part is influenced by the proximity of the other part. Anything can intervene, both in the very protein which makes up the DNA or in the cells to influence the way in which the genes can operate. Irradiation from fallout after the explosion at the Chernobyl nuclear power station has resulted in mutations of human genetic material which in turn has resulted in anything from death to minor physical deformity in people and raised long-term cancer incidence rates. Environmental factors do not necessarily have a lifelong effect and sometimes reversal of circumstances can allow the body to recover.

One of the most difficult issues to resolve is the influence of gender on learning. Gender is clearly genetically determined, yet it appears that most of the differences we can observe in the learning of boys and girls actually have cultural and social origins. Peer, teacher, parental and societal expectations of different roles heavily influence how children and adults behave and even view themselves. For example, various cultural and social explanations of boys' poorer performances are often given, results are scrutinised for gender differences, and teachers and school managers try to compensate for the differences. Single-sex schools or classes are sometimes advocated to ensure equality of opportunity, yet girls develop before boys; puberty occurs earlier, they often talk and read earlier, so it is not surprising that they appear to achieve higher results in external tests for any given age.

It is hard to separate the possible physical differences from cultural ones when differences in outcomes are observed. The effect of male and female hormones, particularly during puberty, must affect learning capability. The mood swings experienced by some girls during menstrual cycles, and even the pain or discomfort experienced at such times, must affect learning effectiveness. Some research does seem to indicate that the female brain functions differently from that of a male, and women are said to be able to multitask better than men, operate on a more emotional level, or mature more quickly. Differences in the ways in which brains are 'wired' may account for some of the gender differences in ways of learning. Certainly, gender is very important to one's identity and society at large; it is usually the first question asked of a mother with a newly born baby.

There are also best times for certain development. Language acquisition appears to be easiest in the pre-school years, when children seem not only to be able to learn their mother tongue, but also to become bilingual or multilingual with more ease. Children seem able to learn to read most quickly between five and seven years of age. It does not mean they cannot learn to read at other times, but the effort they must apply and the teacher must exert to get younger or older children to read is greater. Some of this will be due to the maturation of the brain itself.

The debate is similar to the process/product debate. The environmental influences over a period of time can only work if there is genetically determined material to work on; both are needed, both are influential (see Figure 3.2).

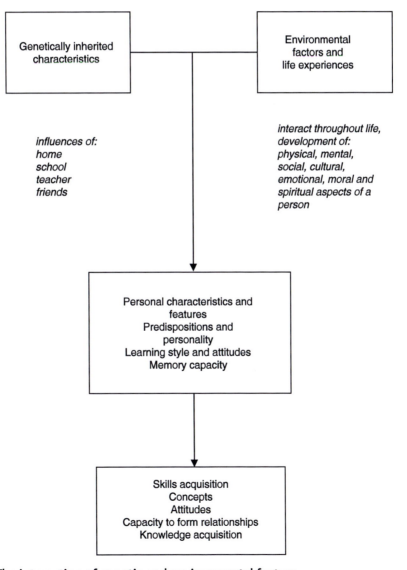

Figure 3.2 The interaction of genetic and environmental factors

The inherited learning tools

Learning may be largely based in the brain, but the sense organs are required to send information to it; the rest of the body carries out the brain's directions, to give us the observed behaviour by which we recognise learning. The whole nervous system is involved. Your brain

> has a trillion brain cells, including:
> 100 billion active nerve cells.
> 900 billion other cells that 'glue', nourish and insulate the active cells.
> Can grow up to 20,000 'branches' on every one of those 100 billion nerve cells.
>
> (Dryden and Vos 1994: 108)

These billions of cells meet up with each other and form enormous networks. Some of the cells connect with each other in the brain, forming these pathways, while others have long branches, enabling them to send or receive messages to and from all parts of the body. The brain pathways are more complicated than any known computer. In living animals, these pathways are in constant electrical action, with chemical changes happening in the cells and between them. Given the number of cells, and the number of possible pathways, the potential for change is mind-blowing, and so is the potential for learning. *The Learning Revolution* (ibid.) has a very readable account of the morphology of the nervous system and its function, with much more detail of brain construction and how different parts of the brain seem to be responsible for different functions.

The brain functions at all sorts of levels to control the things we do. There are the automatic systems which control breathing and heart rate, and are regulated by the hindbrain, which is like a swollen end to the top of the spinal cord. There are the more controllable yet reflex movements such as those that enable us to escape harm. The cerebellum, part of the hindbrain that controls your movements, co-ordination and balance, is important in learning to walk and talk. The middle part of the brain is responsible for memory, emotions, and processing and managing information. The upper part of the brain, the cortex, the bit that looks like an outsize walnut without its shell, has the main thinking parts and personality. The complexity on a gross scale does not stop there. The right and left parts of the cortex do different things and there are pathways between the two sides. Buried inside the midbrain are some important glands whose hormones determine things like our body clock, which then triggers off hormones like the sex hormones, or thyroxine controlling our daily metabolism. All this happens in a mass taking up little more space than a large grapefruit. So you can see how closely linked thinking and our emotions are to controlling other functions of our body.

The physical development of the brain is going to influence what learning can take place, just as physical development of the limbs influences whether walking can take place. With some exceptions and within some limitations, the number of brain cells does not increase as the brain grows, but each cell will grow. There is also a very limited regeneration of the cells if they are damaged. The constant appropriate exercise which brings about such changes is not due to new brain cells growing to replace those lost, as when skin heals or bone knits after a break has been mended, but appears to be due to the ability of the brain messages to find alternative pathways. Some suggest that we should keep up our intake of water between meals to prevent dehydration in the belief that hydration enhances brain function directly, it being largely made up of water. It is difficult to see how this is so, when the electrolyte (chemicals:water ratio) balance is so finely tuned in the brain. It is much more likely that the effect of the dehydration is on general body function, affecting concentration, which in turn affects the brain function. Some schools have encouraged their pupils to carry water in bottles around with them to prevent any possible dehydration. It seems to help.

While an understanding of the biology and biochemistry of the brain is helping us establish the best physical conditions for learning, it still does not address the psychological aspects. Doctors treating people with personality disorders or mental illness use a combination of drugs, psychotherapy and even at times electrical stimulation, although this last is used much less frequently than, say, 50 years ago, when there were few drugs available other than those inducing sleep or hallucinations. Modern therapies take a much more holistic approach to mental illness, recognising that we are complex beings with body, mind and spirit, all of which can become unbalanced in different ways and all of which affect the function of the others. We all live in different social contexts, with different backgrounds, talents and needs. Mental illness is about the malfunctioning of those pathways. Learning problems in children are more likely to be due to impairment of the physical characteristics of the brain. It is difficult sometimes to dissociate the two.

Physical factors affect learning, just as they do any other physical activity. If we are tired or ill, we do not learn as well as normal. Children and young people with a physical disability are liable to have to spend effort and time in dealing with the disability that more able-bodied people can put into intellectual effort. Visual or hearing impairment will prevent access to written or spoken communication. The list is endless and those of you who work with pupils with special educational needs (SEN) of a physical origin will know the kinds of effects these disabilities can have. For these children and young people, the role of a TA is to provide the support that takes away some of the hassle their physical condition elicits, to enable them to use their mental powers to the full. However, in some children, the very lack of physical development of the brain in the womb may have resulted in a reduced number of brain cells, which in turn may prevent full intellectual development.

When categorising children in terms of their SEN, it is tempting to label them in one of the four categories outlined in the SEN Code of Practice (DfES 2001). If their impairment has a clear physical origin like hearing or visual impairment, then it is clear that they have sensory and/or physical needs, but they will also have communication needs. A child with behavioural problems may need emotional and social support, but the behaviour could be due to an inherited gene as is possible in Tourette's syndrome, the condition where the child has an uncontrolled urge to use foul language associated with involuntary tics. Drugs seem to control some behavioural problems, which indicates a chemical imbalance in the brain.

Recent development of scanning techniques has enabled doctors and scientists to study the physical basis of brain functioning while people are still alive. Previously, it was only possible to try to track some of the electrical impulses while people were alive and then study brain tissue after death. Susan Greenfield gave a brief outline of the possible impact of such research in a recent article (Greenfield 2005). She explains that the genetic effect is not stable through life but itself changes, possibly 'switching on and off many times in a lifetime'. She emphasises the importance of environmental stimulation, even on characteristics determined by one isolated gene. She also warns of the growth of a generation experiencing a large amount of 'screen culture', fed streams of mixed bits of information, which will have different learning patterns from our own, with lots of answers, becoming passive receptors of information rather than active learners.

Children with autistic spectrum disorders and Asperger's syndrome, whose brain physiology and chemistry may be different from normal children's, also have different behavioural characteristics. They have compulsive behaviours and find relationships difficult both between other human beings and themselves and between various aspects of the natural world; they cannot make the connections which others can make.

Psychological theories of learning

The brain's basic structure may be determined by genetic factors but, as explained above, this can be influenced right from conception by environmental influences, of which more in the next chapter. Some theories, that abounded 100 years ago, used to suggest that the power of thinking or intelligence was finite, fixed and measurable, hence the development of intelligence quotient (IQ) tests like the Standford-Binet test, favoured in the middle of the twentieth century. There are some inherited parameters, such as can be observed in the inheritance of aptitudes or talents, say in music or dexterity for a craft, but anyone who has looked at family traits knows that such traits can also be encouraged (or discouraged) by the environment in which children are brought up. Identical twins inherit many similar characteristics but can have quite different personalities, which then affect their performance.

Behaviourism

The hindbrain, which controls the more reflex behaviour, is the area that is susceptible to the so-called Pavlovian, behaviourist training. **Pavlov** lived in Russia in the late nineteenth century and worked with dogs. He found that hungry dogs would salivate at sounds or smells associated with food. We all know how we experience this if friends describe a new restaurant or recipe for our favourite food; we do it without thinking, without using the higher order part of the brain – it is a mechanistic reaction.

Thorndike, in America at about the same time, trained cats to use levers to get at their food. We train ourselves to use the clutch and brake to bring a car to an emergency stop when learning to drive. We are at first using our higher order brain, to think about what we are doing, but practising makes it a more reflex activity. **Skinner** worked with pigeons, and recognised that repeating the stimulus strengthened or *reinforced* the connections. The mind, or the thinking part of the brain, is significant, but skills and memory pathways need this kind of reinforcement, and some school learning needs this kind of behaviourist approach with lots of praise and repetition. Skills have to be practised, whether on the piano or the skateboard. Tables and number bonds have to be learnt by repetition to be memorised.

Constructivism

Piaget worked mainly in the 1930s and 1940s. He was a biologist by training but fascinated by his own children whom he observed intensely, recording and commenting in depth on what he found. His work has come under criticism because of his limited area of study, just a few children, but his influence has been profound. Being a biologist, he took a biological developmental view of how thinking or cognitive function develops. He recognised that it develops just like any physical part of the body. It is dependent on both genetic characteristics and interaction with the environment, and it goes through stages. However, he was dogmatic about the stages, saw only one type of development and considered that there was linear progression through the stages. We now appreciate different aspects of learning and thinking develop differently, and the stages are not fixed or as age related as Piaget proposed. Some of the progressivism which took place in schools in the 1960s and 1970s was a misapplication of Piaget's theories, which has been responsible for his ideas dropping out of fashion. Some people thought that all one had to do was to wait for the right stage to come along before teaching certain things: wait and see, offer a rich learning environment and the child's exploration would do all that was necessary for thinking to develop.

His stages of concept development were roughly as follows:

- Up to about 18 months old the infant is involved in developing skills of mobility and sensing his/her environment – the 'sensori-motor stage'.

- Then from 2 to 4 the child is 'pre-operational', only concerned with him- or herself (egocentric).

- By about 4 he or she is 'intuitive' – thinking logically but unaware of what he or she is doing. From 7 to 11 years old, the child can operate logically, but still needs to see and work with real objects to learn and understand – the 'concrete stage'.

- Then the child is capable of 'formal' thinking about things without the 'props' – the 'abstract' stage.

This is why younger children need 'props' for their learning, things like blocks for counting, or artefacts and films about days gone by, yet we know that even young children can have amazing imagination. Piaget ignored the context of learning, and did not ask how to facilitate or accelerate cognitive development. Very young children have all the parts of the brain functioning, formal thinking is possible for them, but the more sensori-motor needs dominate.

Try watching some pre-school children playing together in a good nursery situation. Look particularly for a group without an adult in a 'free play' situation like a play house, or with miniature models – a castle with knights, a sand tray with animals, say, or a water tray with various vessels.

Listen carefully to the dialogue.

You will probably hear adult phrases used as they act out something they can recall.

They may take on different voices as they act a part.

You may hear words intended to organise their peers.

You may also hear words misused as they try out language on each other, where the meaning of words is unclear.

They will be using their hands, feet, eyes and ears constantly.

They may well reason about the enterprise they are engaged in, justifying their activities.

They may question, answer each other, or go and seek adult help.

Putting all of these together you can see that through an activity which is apparently unstructured, children are learning:

how to get along with each other;
how to make sense of things they have heard;
how to learn more words and their use;
how to manipulate objects and tools;
what adults can do;
and more . . .

They are operating on several levels – practical, physical and cognitive, concrete and abstract.

Photograph 3.1   TA using blocks for counting with younger children

Piaget also believed that learning was similar to digestion. We take in food, and digest it to make it part of ourselves. He spoke of 'assimilating' ideas and 'accommodating' them; they then become part of our own mental make-up. He also spoke of 'conservation', recognising certain things still exist even though we cannot see them; the ability of 'operating' internally with 'schemes' or internal working models of how things work or exist. We carry out mental operations with ideas. He believed that children are born without substantive knowledge but have the definite means of coming to know the world. We construct miniature theories of how the world works built up from experiences using our senses; we then are problem solvers – testing strategies or 'schemes'.

> ## An example
>
> Take the way a young child approaches a plate of biscuits. At a first experience the child would take one at random. After several experiences, the child has recognised that colour and texture can determine the taste. He or she will have learnt to choose one with pink icing, or a chocolate layer or avoid the knobbly ones with oats or nuts depending on preferences. He or she has an internal 'scheme' determining action, built up by experiences. Over time this 'scheme' may change, taste preferences might change, or different experiences, such as plastic toy biscuits, might adapt his or her 'scheme'.

Language and background – social constructivism

Chomsky, an American linguist, wrote in the 1950s of the connection between language and thought. He believed that language development was special and not explained as part of general knowledge acquisition.

Bernstein argued that the differences that you can see in children from a range of backgrounds was due to the differing ways that groups of people used language, that people of a 'lower class' or income group might have a restricted vocabulary and grammar structure which in turn could inhibit the mental development of their children. There are still arguments about which comes first, the restricted code of language or the mental capacity to use language. How much is communication necessary to thought? Word language is certainly not the only way to communicate; there are powerful non-verbal ways of communicating, for example a hand gesture or a smile. Body language can create discomfort or raise expectations. Many people appear to 'think' in pictures; I need to draw diagrams, some people need mathematical symbols. We should also recognise that changes of background, language or culture can create barriers to learning.

The social environment

Vygotsky, working in the 1970s and 1980s, believed that the tools or symbols of language enable people to act out within their environment, broadening their horizons, which give added possibilities to their development. While studying children's development like Piaget, he felt we should be considering potential, not what has already developed. Development, he said, lagged behind learning. He also thought that others could assist us in achieving our potential more effectively by working with us than by working alone, as social interaction is part of learning. He described higher mental functions as 'internalised social relationships', and said you could see this in the influence of parents on learning to talk. He particularly developed the concept of a *zone of proximal development* or ZPD and emphasised importance of guidance or collaboration in learning. If we can see the potential learning of pupils with whom we are working we can put in place stepping stones or scaffolding to bring them to the next stage of development, and as the pupils develop 'mastery', external guidance or 'scaffolding' can be reduced. The important thing for the pupil is that the adults provide the scaffolding but do not build the complete tower.

Bruner also used this idea of scaffolding, but added that we can help this process by searching out the patterns and putting the right pieces in place at the right time. By inventing codes and rules, seeking out the regularity and predictability of patterns in knowledge or skills, the teacher/pupil interaction can be speeded up. He emphasised the importance of culture and social interaction but he also acknowledged the constraints of our genetic make-up. He recognised Piaget's stages, but also that they could be accelerated, and that they operated throughout life. He was the main guiding force behind Headstart, an innovative programme for under-fives in the United States in the 1960s. Our current Surestart programme, part of the Children Act 2004, the *Every Child Matters* legislation, is based on much of the Headstart work. It promotes the idea that giving small children a fairer start – pre-school – will give them a surer foundation for later learning.

> **Look at some of the group situations in your school**
> Watch the group and listen as you did with the pre-school group
> Do they concentrate on the task in the same way as the pre-school children? If not – why not?
> Is the talk on the task or about something else – last night's TV programme, the latest Play Station game or what they are going to do at the weekend?
> Do they operate as a group or as individuals sitting together – is the work output a joint product?
> Look at the section on pupils working in groups in *Professional Values and Practice*
> (Watkinson 2005)

Multiple intelligences

Gardner has influenced much recent theory on learning. He suggests that there is not just one intelligence, but multiple strands or aspects, dimensions or domains. There are different intelligences for different things:

- *linguistic:* enables individuals to communicate and make sense of the world through language (e.g. as journalists, novelists and lawyers);
- *logical mathematical:* allows individuals to use and appreciate abstract relations (e.g. scientists, accountants, philosophers);
- *visual spatial:* makes it possible for people to visualise, transform and use spatial information (e.g. architects, sculptors and mechanics);
- *bodily kinaesthetic:* enables people to use high levels of physical movement, control and expression (e.g. athletes, dancers and actors);
- *musical:* allows people to create, communicate and understand meanings made from sound (e.g. composers, singers, musicians);
- *interpersonal:* helps people to recognise and make distinctions about others' feelings and intentions and respond accordingly (e.g. teachers, politicians and sales people);
- *intrapersonal:* enables a capacity for a reflective understanding of others and oneself (e.g. therapists and some forms of artists and religious leaders);
- *naturalist:* allows people to understand and develop the environment (e.g. farmers, gardeners and geologists).

(Pollard 2002: 150)

You can be clever in one area only or in several: verbal/linguistic, logical/mathematical, visual spatial, bodily/kinaesthetic, musical rhythmic, interpersonal and intrapersonal.

Try considering what kind of intelligence you may have
What do you like doing best given a spare hour or two, or a free Saturday afternoon:

reading or writing letters
doing puzzles or working out problems
making things or drawing
active or sporty things
listening to or making music
being with friends
being on your own
or going out of doors?

It is probably a combination of two or more of these.
Would it have made any difference to your life choices if you had considered this before now?

These kinds of ideas have led to labelling children as particular types of learner, and categorising teaching as visual, auditory or kinaesthetic (VAK). This kind of recognition is supposed to enable teachers to tailor their teaching to pupils' needs and thus increase their efficacy. However, the three-pronged VAK approach is proving too simplistic. Pupils need diversity of approach for different subjects, at different stages of their learning. The 'intelligences' approach may be just one way of describing the complexity of the human mind. Certainly some people excel in music, or physical activity, or are good at relating to other people, and it is helpful to recognise these traits and encourage them. But those who do not relate to others may need help in doing so. 'Personalised learning', a buzz phrase popular recently with politicians, should mean trying to understand all children's needs, in the way they learn now and the way they might have to learn in the future, and how to have the tools of learning with them when the teacher is not present.

Emotional intelligence

Linked with the idea of multiple intelligences, yet also linked with the growing knowledge of how the brain functions, is **Goleman**'s theory of the importance of emotional intelligence (Goleman 1996). This was described in the first book of this pair. The links we make with previous experiences, which can have particular feelings associated with them, can affect how we tackle a new topic. We know how stress can immobilise our thinking, and how important attitudes to learning can be. Those who leave school still with an appetite for learning are more likely to succeed in our rapidly changing world.

The cyclical nature of learning

One way of looking at the learning process is that of a cycle of activity, first proposed by **Kolb** (see Figure 3.3).

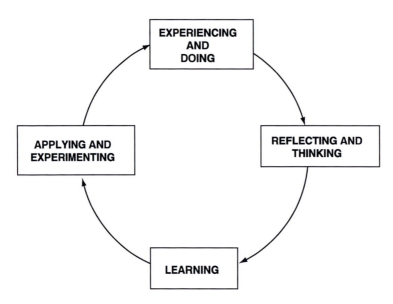

Figure 3.3   A learning cycle

This cycle takes place all the time and many cycles go on at once and are at different stages. Even then, a single act of learning is not as straightforward as this cycle tries to depict; it will be a spiral because of the effect of maturation and the environment, because of interventions and the social context of the learning. The nature of the spiral will change with time. Others have also tried to elaborate the cycle bringing in the effect of emotions on the learning itself, and the changes that take place in a person after learning and reflecting on their learning – in their memory bank or personality or skill base.

Jarvis *et al.* (1998) took episodes of learning, like that described as a task at the beginning of the chapter, and got the learners to try to fit a Kolb learning cycle to it.

> **Try this for yourself**
> Draw a basic learning cycle on a plain sheet of paper.
> Add all the things that influenced you along the way at different points in the cycle.
> Was there an outcome?
> You could end up with something like Figure 3.4

Jarvis also pointed out that we can reject a learning situation so that nothing happens or we might not reflect on what has happened. Much of what we learn is unconscious: skills learning may not involve higher brain function, just repetitive action; memorisation may not involve any reflection, and thus not be useful in other situations. You can see this happen when children learn their spellings, but do not use them in their written work, or are unable to use their tables in an everyday life situation. You can now see how important it is that all the stages in the cycle take place at some time, in order for the learning to make a difference to the learner.

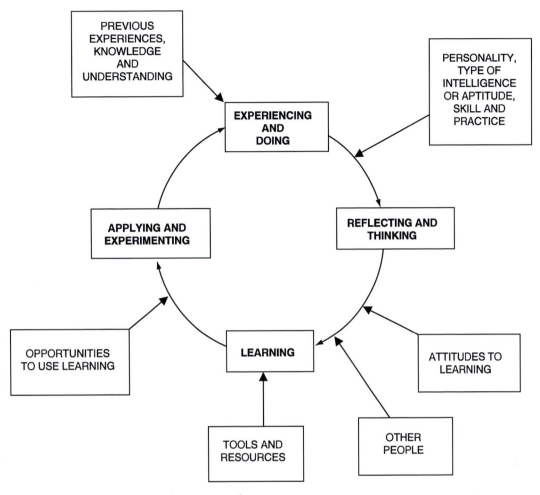

Figure 3.4   A more complex learning cycle

Integrating the theories

You can see that all these theories can represent different ways of looking at the same complex subject, how we think and learn; different theories will support what is happening at different times. The physical mapping of areas of the brain enables a surgeon to predict the effect of any damage to thinking or behaviour he or she might cause when operating for removal of brain tumours. Recent anaesthetic techniques enable him or her to monitor this while operating. It reflects that there is no one way to teach pupils; you need a variety of strategies. Teaching in any one way is boring as well, for both you and the pupil. Following the same mantra each day, because you or the school are convinced that such practice holds the secret way to enhance learning, may well ensure it becomes ignored. Pupils need to become independent learners, with as many strategies for approaching their grown-up world as possible. They need to have the skills of literacy and numeracy, but be able to apply them to other subjects. They may learn best in a quiet atmosphere, but may have to cope with a rowdy one at home. They may excel at football, but will need to organise their resources and budget to exist. Subject matter demands different methodologies and strategies, but so do learners, even individual ones.

Some further reading

Bruce, T. and Meggitt, C. (1996) *Child Care and Education.* London: Hodder and Stoughton (especially Chapter 6, pp. 170–95 and Chapter 9, pp. 261–76 – particularly for those working with the early years).

Bruner, J. S. (1966) *Towards a Theory of Instruction.* Cambridge, MA and London: The Belknap Press of Harvard University Press (theoretical but readable).

Cohen, L., Manion, L. and Morrison, K. (2004) *A Guide to Teaching Practice* (5th edn). London: RoutledgeFalmer (Chapter 10, pp. 167–80 – comprehensive).

If you are interested in the details of Piaget's work and can cope with the jargon, the appendix of Donaldson, M. (1984) *Children's Minds* (London: Fontana Paperbacks) is useful. This book, which constructively criticised his work, was first published in 1978, before other theories came to the fore, particularly those connecting language and thought development and recognising the importance of the context of learning.

Lazear, D. (1994) *Seven Pathways of Learning: Teaching Students and Parents about Multiple Intelligences.* Tucson, AZ: Zephyr Press (practical).

Lee, V. (1990) *Children's Learning in School.* London: Hodder and Stoughton for the Open University (especially part 1, Learning Theories, pp. 3–60).

Muijs, D. (2004) 'Understanding how pupils learn: theories of learning and intelligence', in V. Brooks, I. Abbott and L. Bills (eds) *Preparing to Teach in Secondary Schools.* Maidenhead and New York: Open University Press and McGraw-Hill Education, pp. 45–58. (This is a really useful summary of the many theories and does not relate specifically to older children.)

Pollard, A. (2002) *Reflective Teaching: Effective and Evidence-informed Professional Practice.* London and New York: Continuum (Chapter 7, pp. 133–51).

Smith, A. (1996) *Accelerated Learning in the Classroom.* Stafford: Network Educational Press Ltd (or other books by Alistair Smith) (practical).

Wood, D. (1988) *How Children Think and Learn.* Oxford and Cambridge, MA: Blackwell (especially Chapters 1 and 2, pp. 1–54 – theoretical but readable).

Useful websites

www.acceleratedlearning.com
www.standards.dfes.gov.uk
www.teachernet.gov.uk/teachingandlearning
www.21learn.org

CHAPTER 4

Influences on learning

Physical environmental factors

Diet

We all know that if we are tired or ill we do not learn as well as normal. The diet a mother eats while pregnant, particularly if she lacks certain nutrients, will profoundly affect the foetus. This can retard the normal growth of brain cells as well as other cells. Adequate intake of food and water for growth needs to be maintained throughout life, as the cells are constantly being replaced with new ones. Even the cells of the central nervous system, which have limited powers of re-growth, will undergo chemical changes all through life. The brain cells and associated nerves, functioning through electrical and chemical changes, are especially dependent on an efficient blood supply, which carries, among other things, oxygen. Lack of blood flow to the brain can cause serious brain damage within very few minutes. Proper nutrition ensures maintenance of all the body systems which are necessary for an effective and efficient flow of blood to, round and from the brain.

An area of low employment will have many families on low income, and this is usually accompanied by poor diet. Even free school meals may not supplement the diet, as often the quality of these is not high. The Jamie Oliver programmes on school meal provision highlighted the high fat and carbohydrate content of the meals that were on offer, and after changing this kind of school meal provision to a more balanced diet, teachers indicated that they got a better level of concentration during afternoon school. The government has promised a review of this provision. The fashion for so-called 'junk food' and low levels of exercise has led to concern about the high levels of obesity in children and young people already leading to health risks such as diabetes. The growth of breakfast clubs, used by some families as a babysitting facility, has been due to the recognition that a decent meal at the start of the day helps learning later in the day. This is particularly true if complex carbohydrates are eaten at that time, as the release of energy takes place over a longer period of time without the 'highs' which characteristically follow eating simple carbohydrates like sugar.

Check whether your teacher has ever done a survey of what your class eats for breakfast or as an evening meal. This is often done as part of the Science National Curriculum:

Key Stage 1: Sc2.2c 'that taking exercise and eating the right types and amounts of food help to keep humans healthy'
Key Stage 2: Sc2.2b 'about the need for food for activity and growth, and about the importance of an adequate and varied diet for health'
Key Stage 3: Sc2.2a 'about the need for a balanced diet containing carbohydrates, proteins, fats, minerals, vitamins, fibre and water and about food that are sources of these'
Key Stage 3: Sc2.2d 'that food is used as a fuel during respiration to maintain the body's activity and as a raw material for growth and repair'.

If this has been done, have a look at the results and compare them with the activity levels of the pupils in the class during the day. Discuss this with your teacher.
Have a look at the menus for the school meals. How much of the food is cooked and prepared on the premises? What is the uptake by the pupils of chips or crisps? What alternatives are presented? Consider the diet eaten by some of the pupils and compare it with their afternoon performance. This is a sensitive subject so be discreet; again, discuss this with your teacher.

Exercise, atmosphere and drugs

The air we breathe, which may possibly be polluted by busy local traffic, or low in oxygen because of an oil heater in an unventilated room, is going to affect the oxygen levels in the blood, and thus the function of the brain. Oxygen starvation will cause brain damage to both a foetus and a grown person. Smoking, for instance, with its associated increase in carbon monoxide in the blood, is likely to decrease brain function, and babies born to mothers who smoke are likely to be smaller overall than those born to non-smokers. Taking medically prescribed drugs such as antihistamines can directly affect our concentration and antibiotics often upset our body systems, while some drugs used to help support brain function for conditions such as Alzheimer's or Parkinson's can damage the brain. There is increasing evidence that cannabis, for instance, can cause psychoses in some people, particularly those with a genetic predisposition to mental illness.

It is said that physical activity, stimulating the blood flow round the body, thus bringing more oxygen to the brain, has a speedy and measurable effect on brain function. Certainly, this works if, when nodding off over reading a book, one stops the sedentary activity to take a short brisk walk, even only round the house. It is possible then to resume the more sedentary brain activity with greater concentration. Try taking a class out to run three times round the playground and then try working again. A short active breaktime might do more for subsequent work patterns than the traditional chocolate bar or crisps, but would probably not be acceptable to the pupils!

Comfort, temperature and housing

Discomfort, such as working in a cold room, or sitting on an inappropriate chair to use a computer, has obvious effects on the efficacy with which we learn. Some schools are so convinced of the importance of this they have invested in expensive ergonometrically designed desks and chairs. This move will also help prevent conditions such as backache in later life. We expect children as young as seven to do homework, yet we do not know whether the conditions at home will even provide them a table to work on. The children could be in bed and breakfast accommodation, or part of a family who do not eat at table, so do not have one. It is interesting to see pictures and films of groups of children in some Third World countries, for example, where the children sit in groups on an earth floor, usually under some kind of shade shelter. It will not be easy for those pupils to learn to write with pen or pencil and paper. We also know from our own experience that discomfort because of infection from a cold or a major illness lowers our effectiveness.

We often ask why our main external examination period coincides with what is usually the hottest time of the year – surely it is more difficult to work in extremes of temperature? The answer lies in the traditional school year being set round harvest time centuries ago when most children were needed to help bring in the harvest, so schools were closed for the long break.

Cultural and social factors

Language

Just as the physical environment can affect how we grow and function, cultural and social influences can affect how our learning develops. These influences can be, say, differences in language. This would affect how we communicate, the meaning of words we use. Even for those of us who use English, just look at the differences in vocabulary between the UK and the United States. Children brought up in homes with a restricted vocabulary (Bernstein's theory) would not be able to label and describe as many things as, and express their ideas as well as, those with a wider vocabulary. Similarly, they may use a less complicated grammar structure, which would also limit the way they use their own language. This would stop children developing complicated cognitive concepts to the same extent as those who came from homes that used more words and more complicated ways of talking and expressing themselves. One of the functions of education is to broaden the range of experience, including actual vocabulary for children. It is important to try to distinguish children from such environments from those with a physical impairment or general learning delay. Recognition of the problem gives you ideas immediately of how you can help them in school to communicate.

Looking at restricted vocabularies
Get a copy of the *Sun*, the *Daily Express* and *The Times* for any one day.
Count the number of pages which have news items of any kind.
Find any one news story reported in each paper.
Count the number of words used to describe that item in each paper.
List the number of different nouns or adjectives used in that item.
The range of vocabulary as well as the length of the piece produced by the three newspapers on the same news item are different.

This is different from the editorial choice of article to publish in the paper or the political slant preferred by the paper.
This is an interesting activity to do with pupils of Year 5 upwards.
It would be interesting, but would have to be handled sensitively, to know which families took which paper – or none – daily.

The above paragraphs refer only to pupils speaking and listening to one language. In our increasingly globalised world, there are few schools without at least one family where English is an additional language (EAL). If the second language is learnt in the early years, the lucky person can be bilingual and able to communicate as effectively in two or even more languages. However, frequently the pupil is being taught and expected to communicate in a language less familiar than their own. Again their vocabulary will be restricted, and their fluency slower than their peers'. This is not related to capability and sometimes pupils with EAL can appear to be slow learners, when their problem is language, not intelligence. But, if the pupil is also a slow learner the lack of fluency and understanding will be an additional handicap. It is possible for children to have lived in so many different countries in their short life that they have not established a base language. Understanding and communi-cating simple ideas like colours, learnt largely in infancy by most children, can be major tasks to such pupils. If you work with pupils who have this kind of need, seek specialist help and advice.

Social development

Social interaction or lack of it can affect learning (Vygotsky's theory). This is partly connected to the point about language, but it is also about being able to relate to other people, learn with and from them and communicate as well as possible. Playgroups and nurseries can be invaluable in helping children develop socially before they come into mainstream school, where for so much of their time they are confined to a desk or table. Children need to develop good relationships with those around them, or life may easily become unbearable for them. Children learn about relationships from watching and imitating people around them. The bonding between parents and babies is considered crucial and mothers are encouraged to hold newborn babies from the word 'go', while fathers are encouraged to be present at the baby's birth, not just to be a birthing partner to the mother.

If you do not work with very young children, try spending time in a nursery or playgroup. Watch the children in the role-play areas.
Children will act out what they have seen at home or sometimes on television screens. They will cook and look after other children if that is what happens in their home, or shout at the other children and send one out for a 'takeaway' if that is what they are used to.
Take care when interpreting role-play, as sometimes children act out their fears as well as reality, or scenes from fiction rather than reality.
Always discuss what you see with the staff in the group.

Father figures or male role models in the home are still considered to be significant whether the children are male or female, even in this era of successful one-parent families. Educationalists worry that schools, particularly primary schools, are becoming increasingly female domains. Toys like teddy bears and, for the very young, even a piece of blanket can become a surrogate friend. Many of us have had imaginary friends when little. Bowlby (1965), working for the World Health Organisation after the Second World War, was a significant influence on childcare strategies in early childhood, believing that the mother, or mother figure, was the significant central person in a baby's life. However, while there is a lot of truth in this, it is not only relationships with parents that are important, but also having grandparents, carers, brothers and sisters. It is the quality of the care and of the people that determines their significance and influence. Many babies attend day nurseries successfully from a very early age, but a key worker is usually assigned to them in these stages to ensure that the right sort of bonding and relationships develop.

Children see what happens when they do things that are not allowed, and can behave in several ways, depending on circumstances; by their behaviour, they influence how adults and other children react. Often parents will say to teachers when their child's behaviour at school is described on open evening, 'but he's not like that at home' or 'she's never done that before'.

When children change schools, either because their family has moved house or because of their age, they may have to re-form friendships and teacher–pupil relationships, as well as find their way round a strange building and adjust to different timetables and subjects. All sorts of things affect a child's ability to settle in a new environment. Generally, an unsettled child will be fearful and tearful, but such feelings could manifest in angry, even aggressive, behaviour as the pupil is cross about being put in this strange situation. Pupils with learning problems, a disability or with little ability to communicate either because of their home language being different or through speech problems may have a higher risk of unease with new situations, as they find it more difficult to understand what is happening. But, beware of misinterpreting the reasons for difficult behaviour; always talk matters through with the teacher if you have concerns, and respond as he or she directs. Language that offers choice is helpful, such as, 'shall we do something together or can you do it on your own?' Children choose who they want to be with and do things with; social relationships are a two-way process.

We are not equally sociable: some will always be isolated, happy with their own company; others are gregarious, not comfortable unless surrounded by others. This may depend on our upbringing and experiences, but it may also be a reflection of innate characteristics, that is, whether we have good interpersonal or intrapersonal intelligence. Most of us have times when we want to be alone and times when we need others. As far as learning goes, it is possible to learn in isolation, encouraged, it seems, by the ICT revolution; computer usage encourages lone working as well as a 'screen culture'. There is clear evidence in schools that children have fewer social skills; they have not played card and board games at home, or taken meals as a family. Eating is often finger food or just with a bowl and spoon and takes place in front of the television rather than at a table. Children do not know about taking turns, or using rules for games, or socialising around a meal table, so find such activities in school yet another thing to learn.

The internet and appeal of emailing does enable lone people to communicate. More and more businesses allow their workers to spend time at home working, and some workers make use of their time while commuting on public transport. There is still a need for interaction in order to ensure the most effective learning, that learning off-screen is not just trying to memorise facts or jump through hoops of other people's designs. Video links enable virtual conferences to take place over great distances, but there is still a need for face-to-face dialogue; questioning by the learner and the tutor is very important. Body language as well as verbal language is still needed to explore the full nuances of an intellectual debate.

The growth in popularity of such techniques as circle time helps pupils express their views and fears in public. Some schools set out to teach the rules of debate. Group working, as described in the partner book can enhance learning considerably, provided the activity is appropriate for this and is set up properly.

Different schools, just like different families, have a range of views of what is socially acceptable in a range of circumstances.

Find your school's behaviour policy
What is acceptable in the various situations around school:

classroom
playground
lunch hall
laboratories
toilet areas?

What guidelines are set in individual classrooms for what is acceptable?
What level of noise for what activities is acceptable?
Try monitoring the conversations during group work and discuss these with the teacher concerned.
Is the activity one that should really be done individually in silence?
Is the group work collaborative, demanding conversation on task?
Is the task a low level one where conversation about football or the previous evening's television is acceptable?
What do the pupils talk about at lunchtime?
Do the pupils talk with you at times other than class/teacher driven activities?
What are their major interests and concerns?

Cultural factors

Different cultures will have their own rules or customs of behaviour towards others, and even their own ways of being abusive. Not only will differing languages have different words which are considered offensive, but also gestures which are ordinary to some are obscene to others. It is important that you be sensitive to cultural diversity which is not necessarily racial; even people in different parts of our own country have different understandings. Traditionally, people brought up in the north of England are more open and can seem blunt or even rude to a 'southerner'. The use of cars, higher female employment and commuting have all led to a decrease in local community understanding and support.

Neighbours are less likely to care for each other, or even know of their joys and troubles. Electronic communication rather than meeting people face to face does not help understanding of the ways in which humans can operate as social beings. The growth of fundamentalism, with its seemingly strict and isolationist tenets, may in part be the result of a concern at the loss of traditional values which once supported families and communities.

Disagreements over dietary needs and clothing can cause problems in a school. Food and clothes are seen by families as their responsibility, not the school's: the school should concentrate on the education of the mind! So, cultural differences of opinion, from choice of chocolate bars at breaktime to the wearing of headscarves, can cause more problems in school with parents than changes in the curriculum.

Variations in family values and practices may differentiate pupils' responses. For instance, it may be traditional within a family or group that females never answer before males have had their turn, or that it is not done to contradict a teacher. Thus a pupil may be reluctant to challenge ideas or comments. Homes where books are rare and conversation is limited may influence children to feel that all books are pointless and words are not helpful to express feelings. For them the motivation to learn from the printed word is minimal and problems may be addressed with violence before open discussion.

Moral development appears to come about as part of social and cultural development. Different cultures have moral values and codes of conduct which may differ from those you are used to or those of the school. Where boundaries are clear and whether parents are strict or lenient, even young children know when they are doing 'wrong'. It seems to be natural to challenge boundaries, and if these are flexible or ever-moving, children may experience problems; they know when they have overstepped the mark by the reaction of the one who has set the parameters, yet too great a reaction can result in rebellion. Boundaries that are too different from those experienced at home will create tensions in school, but we want to respect all backgrounds and provide young people with the tools to think for themselves, make their own judgements and decisions. The school needs to provide a clear moral code, yet enable the pupils to be independent thinkers.

The way in which different cultures have differing methods of childcare, whether boys and girls are to be educated together, and in some cultures whether girls are to be educated at all, clearly makes a difference to other development. The kind of clothing, food, art and music which surround a child from the early years will influence development and growth; they are part of the environmental influences on inherited characteristics mentioned earlier in the chapter. The rituals and customs which surround daily life or religious festivals become part of our lives but also influence the kind of person we grow up to be. You must guard against forming stereotypical assumptions that because of a person's gender or apparent ethnic origin, he or she will behave in a certain way or hold certain opinions, yet you should recognise that differences can affect development and access to the curriculum [3.3.7].

It obviously helps the school to understand the background from which their pupils come [1.1b]. Your main objective when working with pupils whose cultural background, dialect or home language is different from your own is to respect it, and recognise and appreciate the additional richness that it brings to school life [3.3.7]; it is about reinforcing their self-image. Their knowledge and understanding of ways different to yours, their food, clothing, art, music and traditions, add a diversity and interest. There will be some school policies about such celebration of cultural diversity, about how various different religious festivals might be observed, how dress codes might be different and where additional resources might be found. This is particularly important where there is a monocultural population as can be found in areas of East Anglia or other largely rural areas. It is difficult to help such pupils understand the richness that has come to the whole country from being a multicultural one, and to stamp out the racism that is evident in such communities.

Personality factors

The cumulative effect of the environmental factors on the genetically determined, inherited factors is what makes up a human being at any one time in his or her life. It is possibly clearer to understand in the more physical manifestations of development. Predisposition to certain diseases, some of the cancers, for instance, may or may not lead to the development of that condition, depending on the environmental factors affecting that person's life. The same is true of personality. An inherited capacity of musical ability in some circumstances may be ignored, while for others it provides an opportunity for developing talent, as well as, in others, becoming a source of irritation. If the teaching is misdirected to the type of musicianship, emphasising reading music notation, say, rather than a wide musical appreciation, the result can be a frustrated and negative individual. For others the reverse could happen. For example, what the child wanted was to perform classical music as written by certain composers, so for him or her sitting and listening was a source of frustration.

Pupils are all individuals, and will grow into distinctive adults responsible not only for their own lives, but probably those of their children or colleagues at work or fellow members of a team. Any of you who are parents or managers will understand the dilemmas that face adults working in schools. You always have to maintain a balance between encouraging or allowing individual wishes against the needs of the family or organisation or your perception of the future. Where there is mutual respect for the role and needs of the other members, such a balance is easier. Even very young children will show their personality in many ways. Your personality will affect the way you work with both the adults and the pupils in your school and it is worth spending time reflecting on facets of your own personality and the kind of contribution you will make to the life of the school. Traits such as extroversion, agreeableness, conscientiousness, neuroticism and openness to new experiences are thought to be measurable, but I have not found out how this is done.

Part of knowing yourself as a teacher is about your values, aims and commitments, subjects dealt with in the partner book, but part of it is about knowing what kind of person you are.

> **What kind of person are you?**
> Are you aware of your prejudices and predilictions?
> Are you a happy person, able to cope with minor troubles in your family circumstances, or are you easily depressed?
> Are you friendly, easy to talk to, able to listen and empathise?
> Do you get flustered if things don't go as you expected them to?

Does the thought of an interview or a test worry you?
Do you get angry at little things?
Do you know what makes you angry?
Have you ever lost your temper, become out of control? What happens?
Would you describe yourself as a loner or gregarious?
Do you know how you learn best?
Do you have a good sense of humour? What makes you laugh?

Knowing yourself as a person and a learner helps you have an insight into the ways of pupils, to establish a rapport with them and empathise with their efforts to learn.

Can you do the above exercise on any of the pupils with whom you work?
It might be useful to talk the list through with them and see what their answers are; they are likely to be different in different contexts.
Ask about when they are at school, with their friends or at home.

Pollard has a simple questionnaire that can be used with pupils, reproduced from Mortimore and colleagues' work in junior schools in London in the 1980s (Pollard 2002: 99), which asks about relationships to other children, anxiety levels, learning habits and behaviour. They tracked children's changes over three years showing how development, different teachers and friends, and changing home backgrounds can all affect the way in which a child behaves and learns in school.

Riding and Rayner (1998) have reviewed a lot of the work round the ways in which children learn, and recognise that 'style' is as complex a concept as personality. They describe four main ways of looking at style, all combining to result in what actually happens in any one person.

Style could consist of:

- the learning processes supposed to be going on in the child. The ways of measuring this are imprecise, depending on what theory of learning is being looked at. Kolb described learners as being reflectors, theorists, pragmatists or activists when operating in the cycle of learning he described.

- the ways people study. While this appears to be more measurable it may or may not relate to the actual learning going on. Learners can be described as focusers, scanners, impulsive or reflective thinkers, or divergent or convergent thinkers.

- how the learner perceives, interacts with and reacts to the learning environment. This will depend on the sort of stimuli a learner responds to. It includes visual, auditory, tactile and kinaesthetic learners.

- cognitive skills, things like short-term and long-term memory development. It assumes learning is an information acquisition and retrieval system. The efficiency with which this works will define how well the learner operates.

What matters is not defining the style closely, but recognising these differences exist in any group you work with, and then trying to adopt teaching approaches to support the most effective learning. Discussion of such ideas with a group of pupils, especially those in secondary school, could be very worth while, getting them to explore how they can work best when on their own, or what kind of support they would benefit from.

Emotional factors

It can be seen from the above that language and culture influence social and emotional development as well as intellectual development. Computers may do better than a single brain in some circumstances, such as multiple calculations, but they have no emotions; they do not feel in the way humans do. Caring for children is not just about provision of food, clothing and a warm home; a child's happiness, ability to cope with misfortune, the security of being loved for oneself are all important. They enable a child to develop satisfactory relationships and use his or her many talents to the full. The concept of 'emotional intelligence' was explored in the last chapter; it really indicates that our emotional state is important in how we think and act.

Motivation

This is one of the greatest influences on learning. The will to achieve can overcome many physical and social handicaps. Some motivation may be associated with the kind of reinforcement activities mentioned in the previous chapter; for example, the rewards of food (sweets?) can be motivators. Other things can be demotivating, like the attitudes of one's friends to learning. If the friends who matter jeer at the pupil who likes to read a book, calling him a 'boffin', it can put him off, often at a crucial period in puberty when revision is needed. It can be a form of bullying. Sometimes a negative comment can motivate a person to try harder, like telling a pupil that a certain aim is impossible. However, this reaction is not predictable and you would be unwise to try it as it could totally demotivate the pupil and prevent them ever trying to achieve that end again. Part of growing up is to become able to put some of these emotions on hold when having to do other things. Younger children are less able to control these emotions and teenagers' hormones play havoc with their control systems.

Wood (1988) points out that we do not always draw the distinction between ability and effort, although some school reports to parents about their child do so. At about 11 years of age, he suggests, children perceive the difference, and it can cause a problem. If they work hard, it may indicate they are of lower ability, having to put in more effort than their friends to achieve the same thing, so some stop trying just at a time when many are going to meet greater competition in the 'big' secondary school. Teachers can unwittingly treat girls and boys differently in the same class, as was observed in mixed gender mathematics lessons. Boys had more negative feedback but it usually commented on things like their inattentiveness, whereas criticism of girls tended to reflect their ability in mathematics. The girls were then more likely to be demoralised, feeling there was nothing they could do to improve. Where self-motivation is not high, teachers' comments can be a powerful demotivator, as many pupils actually do want to please their teacher.

Self-confidence and self-esteem

This can be a global or a specific characteristic. We can have a good self-image generally but a poor view of our capability in sport, for instance, or ability to do mathematics. This also highlights the problem of aligning academic success with intellectual ability and competence, thus a sense of worth; lack of academic achievement can result in a low sense of self-worth. The debate over vocational qualifications versus 'A' levels has actually been going on for years, and there are people who consider those who have skills to be second best to those who can pass tests. Some TAs are classic examples of people lacking in confidence yet oozing with talent; they have experience and understanding in dealing with children, running a home, managing a budget, working with other adults, supporting learning and teaching, yet they may have left schools in their teens with no qualifications to their name. Some of you have had to gain English and mathematics qualifications provide evidence for 2.6, you have sailed through the Learning and Skills Council procedures, yet probably wrote off your abilities because of your own school experiences.

Attention-seeking behaviour can come from pupils' low self-esteem and low self-confidence. They need someone to help them because they do not trust themselves. 'Looked-after' children are particularly vulnerable to such feelings as they have feelings of failure or rejection, having been placed with a family which is not their own. Children from families under stress, from circumstances such as potential eviction or separating parents, will also feel a sense of guilt or rejection, part of the problem in the family, not just a bystander. There is 'evidence that self esteem is related to parental involvement, warmth, expectation, respect for the child and consistency of parenting' (Riding 2002: 7). 'For a child to feel secure and self-controlled two elements are required: (1) . . . security, self-esteem and self worth and (2) a reasonable, consistent and lovingly applied system of discipline and control . . . absence of either is likely to result in problem behaviour being exhibited' (ibid: 8). Later, he points out, peer culture and values will affect self-image. School culture and ethos will have a significant effect on a pupil's emotional state and thus on learning style. There is little the school can do to change the effect of the home, but 'a sensible and sensitive management system in the school is important, (but) the main effect will be due to individual teachers and their personal effectiveness . . .' (Ibid.: 13).

Consider your own schooling
Which members of staff had an effect on you?
Why?
Was it their personality?
Or their understanding of their subject?
Or their ability to put the subject matter across to you?
Or their understanding of your needs?
Then, if you are still in touch with any of your fellow pupils ask them to reflect on the teachers they knew.
Did you all feel the same?
What were the differences?
Talk about what made the differences.

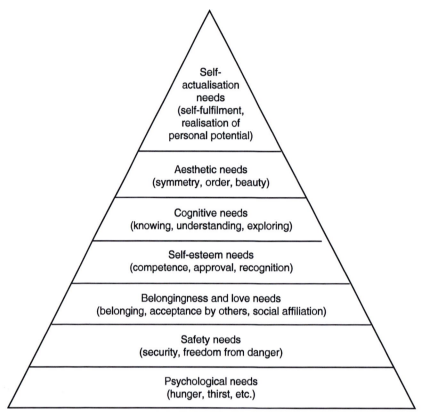

Figure 4.1   Maslow's hierarchy of human needs (Hughes 2004)

Maslow's hierarchy of human needs puts self-esteem needs as more fundamental than cognitive needs, both necessary for self-fulfilment (see Figure 4.1).

In *How Children Fail*, Holt (1964) describes how children can be scared in class when asked a question where they do not know the answer. The trouble is we do not often allow them 'thinking time'. When they are not under pressure they are more likely to come up with the right answer. Unfortunately, examination conditions need speed. Holt felt that many homes and schools destroyed the intellectual and creative capacity of children by the way in which we make them do things, largely by making them afraid. Part of this is presenting ourselves as the all-knowing, all-powerful, always right person. While he advocates only teaching a child what he or she wants to learn and not having a predetermined curriculum, much of what he wrote 40 years ago can make salutary reading. In *How Children Learn*, he emphasises that children do not learn just knowledge, but also curiosity, courage, independence, resourcefulness, resilience, patience, courage, competence and understanding (Holt 1967). He hopes that schools can be places where pupils are not afraid to make mistakes, where they learn to be in control of their own learning, and learn out of interest rather than to appease the adults in power.

Emotional well-being is described in the Early Learning goals in the foundation stage curriculum guidance. Terms used such as trust, safe and secure, consistency, feeling valued and developing a sense of belonging give an indication of what this means. Dowling (2004) reminds us not to have preconceptions about children's sense of grief, which is often great because they do not have years of experience to help them cope, and they may not have words to describe their distress. Small children without words to express their feelings will show their distress or temper in tantrums and their joy or excitement by running round like a mad thing; they also respond to the emotions of those around them. It is not a good thing to protect children from feeling emotion. To be emotionally healthy, they need both to experience a range of emotions and to express themselves in a socially acceptable way.

By the time they are of school age, able to voice their feelings and to understand circumstances, children usually keep tantrums under control. By 7 or 8 they have a concept of the passage of time, and the excitement of anticipation of things like parties or holidays becomes more manageable. By 10 and 11 they are competent to deal with more complex situations without panicking, like finding themselves lost in a shopping centre or falling off their bicycle in a strange place. Children can regress in terms of physical development when they are under emotional stress: toddlers can revert to soiling; primary age children can become bedwetters. The results of the inner conflicts of children going through puberty will have been experienced by many of you as parents. They want to be treated as adults, yet at times they want the security and understanding they had as infants. Moody or withdrawn behaviour can also signify that something is wrong. The increased recognition pupils' need to talk to someone after traumatic events within school life has meant an increased emphasis on the work of counsellors after such an event.

It is important that you recognise such changes for what they are, and know how to manage them. You need to think about what causes emotional distress, things like changed circumstances or a fluctuating stability at home, changing boundaries, people or places. Pupils with SEN or EAL may find it more difficult to understand what is happening and therefore find it more difficult to adjust to such changes; it is also important to realise that a totally cosy, secure, unchallenging environment may also not be helpful to learning. A state of no stress creates a state of relaxation, and dependency on the provider of the environment. Too much stress clearly has a negative effect; what is required is a balance between high challenge and low threat.

Spiritual development and needs

We all experience something that is part of our inner self but is difficult to define. Some of you will be in faith schools where any discussion of spirituality will be confined to the religious beliefs and values associated with the foundation of the school. But spiritual development is not confined to the development of religious belief or participation in the practice of a particular faith; it is about experiencing wonder and joy, seeking the meaning of things, wanting a purpose for them. Children appreciate straight but sensitive talking from adults, although many adults will feel that they need help in talking with children about such matters. As they grow up, children begin to sort out legends and myths from factual evidence, for instance when reading Harry Potter books or *The Lord of the Rings*.

We all tend to fight shy of discussing deep feelings about spiritual matters, unless we feel really sure of the people we are with. Yet the very depth of these feelings shows how important they are to the human condition. You need to consider these feelings when trying to understand the pupils you work with and welcome any opportunity to discuss such matters if they arise.

Try reading the Ofsted handbook guidance on the development of pupils' attitudes, values and other personal qualities. The judgement pages give descriptions of behaviour, which reflect attitudes (Table 8, p. 52; Table 9, p. 56).
Ask yourself the questions which inspectors consider:

Do pupils show an interest in school life, and the range of activities the school provides?
How well do pupils behave in lessons and about the school?
To what extent are pupils enterprising and willing to take responsibility?
Do pupils form constructive relationships with others?
Are pupils free from bullying, racism and other forms of harassment?
Does the school promote good relationships, including racial harmony?
How well does the school deal with incidents such as bullying, racism and other forms of harassment?
To what extent do the pupils have confidence and self-esteem?
Does the school stimulate in pupils a desire to learn?
To what extent does the school set high expectations of pupils' conduct and successfully implement policies to achieve them?
How well do pupils develop self-knowledge and spiritual awareness?
How well do pupils understand and respect other people's feelings, values and beliefs?
How well do pupils understand and apply the principles that help distinguish right from wrong?
How well do pupils understand and fulfil the responsibilities of living in a community?
How well do pupils appreciate their own and other cultural traditions?

See the primary handbook for further questions (pp. 52–8).

The fact that so much is put into an inspection framework aimed mainly at looking at standards of school work shows the importance of such issues to the learning of the pupils in the school.

Essential reading

The sections in the relevant NC for the age group with which you work on personal, social and health education (PSHE).

DfEE and QCA (1999a) *The National Curriculum: Handbook for Primary Teachers in England; Key Stages 1 and 2.* London: Department for Education and Employment and Qualifications and Curriculum Authority, pp. 136–41.

DfEE and QCA (1999b) *The National Curriculum: Handbook for Primary Teachers in England; Key Stages 3 and 4.* London: Department for Education and Employment and Qualifications and Curriculum Authority, pp. 188–94.

Some further reading

Dowling, M. (2004) 'Emotional wellbeing', in L. Miller and J. Devereux (eds) *Supporting Children's Learning in the Early Years.* London: David Fulton Publishers.

Holt, J. (1964) *How Children Fail.* London: Penguin Books. (This was a very influential little book in the late 1960s in helping teachers recognise the potential damage they can cause.)

Holt, J. (1967) *How Children Learn.* London: Penguin Books.

Hughes, P. (2004) 'Learning and teaching: what's your style', in C. Bold (ed.) *Supporting Learning and Teaching.* London: David Fulton Publishers, pp. 34–49.

Pollard, A. (2002) *Reflective Teaching: Effective and Evidence-Informed Professional Practice*. London and New York: Continuum (especially Chapter 7, pp. 152–8 and Chapter 15 on social inclusion, pp. 339–56).

SCAA (1995) *Spiritual and Moral Development*. London: School Curriculum and Assessment Authority.

SCAA (1996) *Education for Adult Life: The Spiritual and Moral Development of Young People* (Discussion Papers: No 6). London: School Curriculum and Assessment Authority.

CHAPTER 5

Strategies to support learning

From theory to practice

The last two chapters looked at the complexity of the learning process and what affects it. So what can you do about the issues raised? Without getting involved in the more direct act of instruction you can and have been supporting pupils' learning by all that you do in school. We now recognise that just reacting to pupils is not enough although in the 1960s and 1970s there were some people who thought that this was all one had to do to educate children. If the environment was designed in the right way and children were tracked through it, they would learn all they needed. The most famous example was the school in Suffolk called Summerhill, started by A. S. Neill (Neill 1962). It still exists. Lessons were optional, the main hallmark of the school was freedom; pupils could take examinations if they wanted to. The growth of the ideas of freedom, discovering knowledge and allowing children to develop had grown through the twentieth century for several reasons. The ideas of the psychologists described in Chapter 3 became more widely known, but it was also more widely recognised that adverse social and emotional conditions as described in the last chapter prevented children from growing, not only physically but also intellectually.

The philosophy of people like Schiller (Griffin-Beale 1979), an inspector of schools in the early part of the twentieth century, had been influential in making teachers question the traditional methods of 'talk and chalk'. He challenged the social conditions in which children were brought up and introduced ideas of 'learning by doing' into the classroom. He championed ideas like developing creativity in children, not just filling them up with facts. The nursery movement, inspired by people like Susan Isaacs (Isaacs 1929) and Rachel Macmillan, pioneered ways of working with young children where they learnt intellectually through play and also developed a healthy body. The provisions for play were inside and outside (fresh air and exercise being important for physical health, especially in slum areas) and stimulated intellectual, social, emotional, moral and spiritual development. Sybil Marshall's account of how she used these kinds of ideas in her small Cambridgeshire primary school was compulsory reading when I did my teacher training in the early 1970s (Marshall 1963). If you read any of these accounts or parts of them, you might recognise some of the descriptions from your own schooling – it depends how old you are.

In schools where structure and good teaching remained alongside the creative, under-standing environment, children flourished and such schools became international beacons for good practice. The Plowden Report of a large survey of primary schools celebrated such schools (Plowden 1967). But the report has often been blamed for encouraging the growth of 'progressive' ideas of schooling where the provision of a safe but stimulating environment was all that was required. This was not the case. Misinterpretation of the report, of the ideals of the movement for more understanding of how children learn, resulted in schools where the structured curriculum became buried. Children were not challenged, intellectual expectations were low, and academic standards fell. Yet during this period, there were many innovative curricular developments. The Nuffield Foundation looked into the teaching of science in primary schools, and started a movement for building the practical investigative work, nature study and the like into a structured approach on which secondary science could be built (Nuffield Primary Science 1967). A Schools' Council investigated and developed many helpful ideas for teachers, Her Majesty's Inspectorate (HMI) began producing helpful surveys of their findings in school, and commentary on education as they observed it during the 1980s, but it was not enough. Nothing was compulsory and still many children slipped through the net. Some schools provided a limited curriculum and others a broad but superficial one. The late 1980s saw the introduction of a compulsory curriculum for all state schools, ensuring an entitlement for all pupils to a breadth of subjects. Inspection was greatly strengthened and in the 1990s teaching methods in English and mathematics became virtually mandatory. In fact, the Literacy and Numeracy Hours are only advisory, although inspectors must ensure standards are maintained if the strategies are not followed.

You can see the pendulum swings from formal instruction to freedom back to formal instruction. Now, with the new Primary Strategy, comes the recognition that extremes of either do not promote either the highest standards of academic subjects or the best climate for learning [2.9]. Children need the right environment to learn, allied with the entitlement to a rich and varied curriculum and appropriate methods of teaching for both. Unfortunately, the rigid testing regime, with associated inspections and league tables, tends to drive schools down paths that do not provide the broadest opportunities for learning. Understanding the key factors of how children learn is, however, a standard required of HLTAs [2.5]. While following the strategies and methods required by your school or a particular classroom teacher, you must bear in mind those factors described in the last two chapters, and try to incorporate some of the following ideas as you teach.

Allied to these general theories on learning and what affects it, is the understanding of pupils' individual needs. There are many books dealing with these needs ranging from those who have profound and multiple difficulties to those who are gifted and talented. It is not the intention of this book to deal with these but they must not be forgotten.

The physical learning environment

There may not be a lot you can do directly to influence the physical environment in which the pupils with whom you work are growing up, but you should be aware of it. The previous chapter asked whether you knew if your pupils ate breakfast. Do they play out of doors? What do they do in the evenings or holidays? You may have time to get involved with out-of-school activities, whether associated with your school or not; sometimes, this can be a practical way of showing that you care about what happens, but more often you are likely to be busy trying to support your family, run a job, and now study to further your career. Talk with your pupils about their views and why they hold them. You must respect theirs, but they must also respect yours.

The surroundings in which learning takes place in school will influence the quality of the learning. The unspoken messages which the school environment gives to visitors, especially parents, also influences attitudes to the physical environment in general.

An example of good practice

A school in a difficult area of a London overspill town was built in the late 1960s at a time of rapid building, with many prefabricated parts. It suffered a lot of wear and tear over the years. With falling rolls and many changes in staff, and falling employment rates in the parents, morale became low in staff and pupils. The building, equipment and even the school grounds suffered. Local management, with the school getting its own budget, was no help. The governors were largely from the parent body and were having problems with their own budgets, let alone a school's. The school developed a large underspend in its budget. Some items were purchased like books and computers, but such was the vandalism in the area that staff were reluctant to buy more; it was all too much hassle sorting out the mess in the morning. The cleaning was superficial, the toilets began to smell. It became difficult to recruit new teachers as members of staff left.

Parents who cared opted for other local schools for their children.

The head left for another job abroad, and the governors had considerable difficulty in replacing him. The deputy head went on sick leave through stress. The behaviour became more uncontrollable, standards plummeted and despite attempts to prop up the system by the Local Education Authority (LEA), the school failed its inspection. At last the governors agreed to a temporary head, supplied by the LEA.

Where to start? She started with the fabric of the school. She used that underspend and more, gleaned from the LEA special emergency funds. She got builders in to sort the toilets; she started painting areas herself, with one or two governors who understood what she was up to. She was later joined by a few parents. She spent money on good furniture, bright boxes to store equipment. There was resentment among the staff. They did not want to be organised, or organise their rooms. They might be expected to do some painting themselves! She tackled her office first – that too caused resentment! She personally could not work in a disorganised, dingy area. She then dealt with the reception area and the staffroom – 'What about the children?' was the cry. But, the staff appreciated the refrigerator and the microwave. The parents felt more welcomed to the school. She opened the stock cupboard to free access, but kept it well stocked. Alongside this went some straight talking to all staff about her intentions. It was important to get the caretaker and cleaners on board, and other support staff – they could all help in the physical environment.

The playground and outside resources area, long neglected, were not left out. Gradually, over the year she was in post she raised the standards of the physical learning environment and in so doing raised the morale of staff and the prospects for learning of the pupils. Attitudes to learning changed among staff and pupils. Absenteeism of both staff and pupils dropped and infections decreased, as did levels of stress. Change and continuing professional development (CPD) were no longer terms to be feared and objected to out of hand. Parents felt welcomed and began to share their problems with teachers and the head.

The governors were able to appoint a substantive head for the following year who continued the work started. The school standards began to rise again; the school eventually recovered its self-respect and popularity in the community.

The teacher will set the scene of his or her classroom, creating resource centres, setting out the furniture appropriately and putting up displays to create the atmosphere he or she feels is most conducive to the tasks to be performed there. If you are involved in the planning with the teacher, discuss this aspect of the teaching as well as what needs to be covered and how. You may have had, or may still have, a part in maintaining the environment. If possible, you will need to be able to adjust any working environment to provide appropriate lighting, heating or ventilation, and you must make sure the pupils you are with are safe, can move about adequately if they have to, and use the space appropriately [3.3.8]. Remember any security checks when you leave the room, like locking up certain items or closing windows. Your practice in maintaining a personal tidy, organised work area, with the proper tools decently maintained, from paper and pencils to large expensive equipment, will give a powerful example to the pupils. You know yourself that having things where you know where you can find them, materials or tools, makes a job easier. Check BEFORE a lesson that you have correct and sufficient materials for a task; NEVER leave your pupils to go to get something. If you have an emergency, send someone to get help with a note. Even a four-year-old should be able to do this for you.

The Primary Strategy CPD publication *Creating a Learning Culture: Conditions for Learning* (DfES 2004b) has some simple suggestions for considering the physical environment and refers the practitioner to clips in the video material supplied with the books. Kyriacou (1998) has a useful few pages on classroom appearance and he includes personal appearance in his list. There may be a dress code for staff in your school; if so, adhere to it. The era of scruffy teachers has gone. Dress conveys messages just like surroundings. Check also when and where pupils' uniforms should be corrected. Well-established routines and conventions which are consistently applied by all staff do make for a more orderly environment. Elton (1989) refers to the importance of controlling litter and graffiti, repairing damage as quickly as possible, and the importance of attractive displays of pupils' work, which has, traditionally, been particularly neglected in secondary schools. It is noticeable, from visiting schools over a period of years, how this has improved in some secondary schools, yet others still have chewing gum spots on the floor and shabby, badly kept premises.

If you are in a secondary school, it is harder to have any influence over the physical environment; the sheer size of the place and the ways in which the timetable is organised means any one person's influence is limited. Nevertheless, you should try to make your voice heard if you have concerns about the general cleanliness or tidiness in the school and discuss individual concerns about rooms with the teacher responsible. You will find it hard to teach in someone else's room if it is untidy, disorganised or even dirty. Talk with the pupils about the conditions in their toilets, and the food they eat at lunchtimes.

Titman (1994) researched pupils' views on school grounds and found they conveyed many hidden 'messages and meanings which influence their attitude and behaviour in a variety of ways' (p. 63). They 'read lack of care and maintenance as a reflection of their own lack of value to the school' (p. 53).

Display

Whatever is displayed on school walls and the manner in which it is displayed gives messages to pupils and adults about what is valued. If displays become faded and tatty, the message is 'who cares?' Make sure that some of the work you do with pupils is included in displays, consulting the teacher, of course, otherwise the pupils will view their work with you as second best, not worthy of a full effort like that set by the teacher in charge.

> Look at displays in shop windows, art galleries, museums, advertisements and libraries, areas in hotels and restaurants and you will see how differently they convey the messages of their environments.
> Where do you feel comfortable and welcomed?
> Where do you feel relaxed and informal and possibly more careless?

The emotional learning environment

There is now a 'healthy school' project in many areas, under the umbrella heading of the National Healthy Schools Programme (www.wiredforhealth.co.uk). It is not, however, just about having a clean, hygienic and safe school, but also about the good relationships between those who work there to provide a good working climate. Schools are asked to provide evidence in the core themes using a whole school approach involving the whole school community:

- **personal, social and health education** including sex and relationships education, drug education (including alcohol, tobacco and volatile substance abuse);
- **healthy eating**
- **physical activity**
- **emotional health and wellbeing** (including bullying) (DfES and DH 2005: 4).

This latter is described further as being 'to help pupils understand and express their feelings and build their confidence and emotional resilience and therefore their capacity to learn (ibid.: 9). There is growing evidence that participation in such projects by primary schools is resulting in raised standards at KS2.

Questionnaires are sent to all sections of the school community asking participants to rate various items on a five-point scale. The results are collated and compared, and form part of the information feeding into the school development (or improvement) plan (SDP or SIP). Questions range from ones about the fabric of the building and school meals to issues of bullying or communication about work, and access to relevant staff by parents or pupils, things that concern or please people. The differences in perceptions of staff and parents are often interesting.

Pastoral systems

In some schools, particularly larger ones, certain staff have special pastoral roles, over and above the part played by most class teachers. In primary schools it is relatively easy for a teacher to know and understand what may be troubling a child, but in secondary schools form tutors rarely have more than one or two sessions a week with their tutorial group.

Tracking pupils as they change years in a secondary school can also be problematic unless the communication and recording systems operate well. Sometimes a house system is in place and pupils are allocated to one tutor for the whole of their time in the school, whose role is to maintain communication with pupils and parents to ensure no one gets lost emotionally. It can be a daunting task in a large comprehensive of over 1,000 pupils, constantly on the move from room to room. Pupils can even get lost physically in their early days at the school. The tracking of pupils with SEN is usually very effective, but there is a danger of the majority of other pupils being left to their own devices if systems are not in place.

Check on the pastoral systems in your school
What is considered to be part of the role?
Who is responsible for personal, social and health education (PSHE) in the school?
Is the 'hidden curriculum' ever mentioned? If so, when, where and about what?
Do you ever go to assembly? What happens there?
What kind of counselling systems operate in the school?
You may well be told personal information about a pupil – who else should know about it? If it is a serious matter which could affect the well-being of the pupil for more than a day, should this be recorded?
What do you do if you discover incidents of bullying?
Where are the boundaries between you and the class teacher about investigating problems, e.g. incomplete or inadequate homework, apparent unexplained changes in mood in class?
Do you know who is in charge of pastoral care in the school? Is there a policy? How does it operate?
Do you know the named person for Child Protection issues?
Ensure you have a copy of the Child Protection policy of your school and regularly attend any training offered.
If you have any concerns about any of these kind of issues and how they are dealt with, discuss it with a teacher with whom you work closely, a mentor, and, if necessary, with a senior manager.

It is possible that you may have to stand in for a tutorial session in the school as well as for a timetabled curriculum subject. You should prepare yourself for this and follow the teacher's planning in the same way as for a subject lesson, so do consider this in your planning discussions with teachers. Also, as part of the planning, consider any pastoral issues that might arise when you take a particular group of pupils.

The rewards and sanctions or punishment system in your school can also be a useful tool in supporting good emotional health [2.9]. If this is fair and applied consistently by all staff, pupils know that things like racism, intolerance and bullying will be dealt with appropriately. This gives pupils a feeling of security akin to the provision of a safe and secure building. Access to reasonable and fair adults who listen could be crucial for a pupil in distress. The true story *Ahead of the Class* (Stubbs 2003) is about the recovery of a failing school in London following the tragic death of the head by a stabbing, after he tried to protect a pupil. The temporary head insisted, against the odds, that the final year should celebrate their leaving with a 'posh' hotel dinner dance, a 'prom'. It showed how such events, apparently unlinked to the curriculum, can affect how people feel about an organisation or an institution, both staff and pupils.

Self-confidence and self-esteem

This issue was dealt with at some length in the earlier books for teaching assistants (TAs), as it is so important. Hopefully, the chapters on the importance of intrapersonal skills and emotional development will have alerted you to the role this plays in learning. While this material will not be repeated here, do consider the list of page references from Fox (2001), Hook and Vass (2000), and Watkinson (2003b) at the end of the chapter and ensure you incorporate relevant approaches in your work with pupils of all ages.

Some of the strategies suggested for raising self esteem in the classroom
- Talking to everyone the same way, regardless of gender, race or background
- Addressing pupils by their preferred name
- Using positive comments: 'thank you for walking', 'well done for being quiet', including written comments if you can: 'well read today', 'I liked the story'
- Using praise appropriately, not indiscriminately
- Treating boys and girls equally, whether for tasks or treats or even lining up
- Providing a good role model in gender, culture and disability, both in reality and when finding examples in teaching materials such as books and magazines
- Using rewards, praise and congratulation systems for work, including showing it to other staff
- Catching them being good or working hard, and telling them
- Setting small achievable targets and congratulating them on achieving them
- Having reward systems for behaviour; telling the teachers about the good as well as the troublesome
- Valuing work by ensuring it is taken care of, and presented well, by both you and the pupil
- Encouraging independence appropriate to age and maturity
- Enabling and encouraging peer tutoring
- Careful use of humour
- Encouraging children to value their own performance
- Listening to the views of pupils and acting on them where possible
- Avoiding being patronising or sarcastic as pupils recognise both.

Can you add to this?

(Watkinson 2002: 23)

Motivation and inspiration

Kyriacou talks of classroom climate rather than environment to include the emotional side of things which influences learning. He describes three differing kinds of motivation which can be considered: extrinsic, intrinsic and expectation for success. Extrinsic is the sort that responds to obvious rewards, from material rewards to praise, even the awarding of qualifications. People engage in activity because they can see an end result. Intrinsic is the less tangible side of motivation, probably the reason why you are a TA – you get enjoyment and satisfaction from your job. Some pupils really enjoy certain subjects or activities so they will work hard in them even though they may not lead anywhere. The expectation of success is why people persist at doing something even though it may be difficult. If pupils perceive that they cannot do something and really believe that however hard they try, it is pointless, they won't try. Bear these things in mind when setting activities and tasks for pupils; Listen to pupils; note their interests and build on them [3.3.1].

The social and cultural learning environment – planning for inclusion

The major movement towards inclusion over the last decade sometimes seems to be focused on issues of inherited special learning needs, largely caused by genetic 'defects' or problems experienced during pregnancy and birth. Many of them stem, however, from historical ways of dealing with people who are different. Even within living memory society excluded those who they thought were 'barmy' or 'backward'. Some cultures still exclude females from educational and career opportunities. Even with our equal opportunities legislation, the so-called 'top' jobs still have a higher percentage of male members; racism may be legislated against but is still reckoned to be 'institutional' in many walks of life; ageism may be something TAs have experienced in trying to gain admittance to certain learning establishments in the past, although this is decreasing.

The way in which you organise your classroom activities can give out very powerful messages about social inclusion [3.3.3].

Questions to ask yourself
Do I know about the cultural backgrounds and sensitivities of the families whose children come to my school?
Am I clear about the ethos and values which my school stands for and my role within them?
Is there any conflict between my belief systems and that promoted by my school? What can I do about this?
What do I do when pupils ask me about my feelings or beliefs?
To whom can I go in the school to discuss any problems which may arise when dealing with pupils?
What does the religious education (RE) policy for my school contain? Or the policy for collective worship?

The way in which you deal with pupils, ensuring there is no discrimination on grounds of gender, race or ethnicity, will set an ethos of trust and support [3.3.2]. Allow the pupils themselves to voice their feelings on arrangements or make suggestions that can empower them, encouraging a more democratic and open culture within the classroom; encourage co-operation. Cohen *et al.* (2004) categorise their suggestions for promoting inclusion at three levels: structural, interpersonal and personal.

- The structural approach deals with looking at how the teaching of the curriculum can both avoid racial or sexual stereotyping and promote positive images of exclusive aspects of learning. The choice of material for study is influential; history or geography, for instance, can be very anglocentric or eurocentric, yet it is important for all pupils of all races to understand the development of the culture in which they find themselves. The use of source materials for art or design technology, and the use of literature, artefacts or music to support any area of the curriculum can celebrate diversity rather than a particular culture. It is as important for all-white schools as for multi-ethnic schools that there be a recognition of the diversity of different communities.

- The interpersonal approach is about the way in which pupils and adults treat each other, the kinds of motivation and attention to matters of self-esteem and self-worth, of trust and respect. Drama, debates and discussions are essential elements of the pedagogy required to support this kind of approach. Totally teacher-dominated discourse will not succeed in winning the hearts and minds of pupils.

- The personal level is about specific strategies to address matters of self-awareness, develop autonomy and independent learning habits, and to make sure that individual students value their own worth and that of the community from which they come.

Differentiation for individual needs

The ways of working with pupils in groups were described in the first book in this pair as were the ways in which pupils can be grouped. Inclusion within a classroom as well as a school must be considered, so vary your groupings according to needs. This should not always be according to ability as pupils very soon believe they are to perform at the level to which they are allocated. Setting may seem a convenient way of planning but it has social and emotional repercussions; pupils must be seen to have worth. Space and resources can determine grouping. The nature of the task to be performed, whether it is practice, just requiring verbal communication, or needing technical support or adult intervention will influence your decisions. You would be unwise to put together deliberately two pupils known to have mutual antipathy, unless you take care to monitor the results, and deal with any problems; grouping can be used to break down prejudice and discrimination, as well as to separate.

Your decisions will be mostly determined by the patterns set by the class teacher. Unless left entirely to your own devices, you should discuss any proposals before you undertake them, and then monitor them and report back to the teacher the success or otherwise of your actions, discussions and groupings.

Promoting independent learning – developing learning styles and habits

It is important that pupils do not become dependent on the teacher or TA. Hayes (2000) has some useful sugggestions for promoting healthy attitudes to learning:

1. Use flexible teaching methods.
2. Encourage pupils' independence.
3. Recognise that most children do their best.

4. Take failure and disappointment in your stride.
5. Ensure that children have opportunities to clarify points.
6. Encourage children to help one another.

Consider a recent topic you have been following with a pupil or group of pupils. Can you answer these questions about their learning?

Why did you start it?
What did you need to help you: books; an instructor; discussion with other people; time on your own; the right tools or machine; practice?
What strategies, if any, did you include to ensure all pupils felt part of the lesson?
Did the pupils recognise what you did?
What questions did they raise?
Do you or the pupils need to make any changes in the way you work together?
Can you help your pupils understand their own learning styles better?
Which pupils enjoyed the topic and which seemed resentful?
What went wrong? Why?
What went well? Why?
Did the pupils' views matter?
Can you still improve?
Would you do anything differently next time?

Hayes' tips for promoting independence are useful:

Ensure that you:
- offer clear guidelines for behaviour
- make explicit your expectations about work standards
- praise and approve instances of pupil initiative
- demonstrate a willingness to trust pupils' judgements
- accept pupils' errors as a necessary part of the process.

Ensure that pupils:
- know the location of key resources
- understand how to use equipment
- try things for themselves before seeking advice
- accept responsibility for their own actions
- keep their work areas and book trays in good order
- evaluate their own standards of attainment.

(Hayes 2000)

Strategies which support various theories of learning

You need to consider how children and young people vary from one another, in all aspects of their inherited characteristics and their development [2.8]. Consideration of these differences ensures that your methods of support meet their needs. Again, other books describe particular special needs and ways to help; try the David Fulton website or catalogue for a long list of titles on specific learning needs and useful support strategies.

The increased focus on brain research has led to renewed interest in how understanding brain function can be used in teaching. Scoffham (2003) lists 15 possible implications for teaching related to what we know about the brain, and some of them crop up in other contexts:

- Choose a variety of entry points and try to identify broad teaching objectives for each topic, rather than step-by-step stages.
- Use whole class instruction judiciously and explore ways of differentiating activities for different ages and abilities.
- Lessons where children have to listen to the teacher for long periods without a break could be counter-productive.
- We need to discover children's existing knowledge and abilities and tailor our teaching to this.
- Provide children with practical activities and first hand experiences and encourage them to take charge of their learning.
- It may be best to use a variety of learning strategies, especially fieldwork and real world environments.
- Use enquiry questions to draw children into a problem so they then restate them.
- Find out about real-life problems and getting pupils to make models and plans as well as written reports.
- Help children to identify questions and strong personal goals which they think are meaningful.
- Give pupils plenty of opportunities to reinforce their learning by presenting it in different ways, e.g. by teaching a peer, role play, writing a journal.
- Explore ways of transferring concepts from one situation to speed learning.
- Provide pupils with material that is appropriate to their interests and which they can relate to personally.
- Try to create a supportive classroom environment and use techniques such as team building that develop self-esteem.
- We need to acknowledge the differences between the sexes, as well as providing equal opportunities.
- We need to pay good attention to pupils' social, spiritual, emotional and physical well-being.

(Scoffham 2003: 57)

While some of the various theories about learning seem to indicate a set inherited intelligence, many people not only have ensured the best climate and environment for learning but also have attempted to accelerate the process itself. As there are many theories, all have a value in different contexts, and using the various theories can suit differing purposes. You must determine the kind of learning you are trying to promote and which theory best fits the circumstance, then you can adapt your methods accordingly. The suggestions below follow the order in which the theories were introduced in Chapter 3.

Using behaviourist theories

There is a need to practise some learning, particularly skills, and if success is associated with reward, it can be a powerful motivator to help learning. PE and music are obvious subjects which require skills practice, but learning tables or spellings also fall into this category. Finding different ways to do the same thing, to stop the repetition being boring, is one of the strategies to help this kind of learning. Breaking down the tasks into even smaller steps for some pupils will help, and the reward is getting them to recognise that achieving each small step is a milestone for them. Usually a 'well done' is sufficient reward, but stickers, housepoints or even outings or other treats can be used. Just make sure you are doing what the class teacher would have done, and keep within the rewards systems of the school [3.3.4].

Target setting with pupils depends on just this strategy – aiming and then achieving can be very satisfying for both you and the pupils. These can be personal behaviour targets, Individual Education Plan (IEP) targets, or targets set as part of marking work.

Using constructivist theories

The correlation of stages of mental development, more particularly the knowledge or cognitive development, with physical development makes a lot of sense; we do not expect children to run races before they walk. We need to present children with ideas and facts in stages and give them props and practical experiences. We must give time and thought to the 'play' of children, and allow their brains time to assimilate and adapt as we give time for muscles to develop in running.

Much of the understanding of the value of play came from the work of people like Piaget. So, early learning for the two- to four-year-old is practical and experience based, some even say 'science based'. Children explore and investigate naturally, and begin to make sense of the world around them. Many teachers brought up through early years practice still believe that structured play would be the best way to support learning up to six or seven years old; indeed, many continental kindergartens do just that. Children need to experience the world to make sense of it, to put meaning to the words they use, before they can make sense of reading and writing and counting; then they come easily to the more abstract coding of letters and numbers, which we use in formal lessons.

We all need to learn some factual knowledge, and the facts must be absorbed and digested like food taken into the blood. If they remain undigested, or unassimilated, they are not usable or applicable in other areas of knowledge. It is no good just knowing your tables or how to spell, essential as these skills are, if you cannot use them, and this is where some kind of activity following a teacher input is needed. The main part of most lessons is in fact spent practising and reinforcing the teacher input. If this can be done in a way which shows pupils a wider application than that given by the teacher, they will form their own 'construct' of what is to be learnt. Only they can do this, we cannot learn for them; learning is an active pursuit, not a passive absorption exercise.

Sometimes, as children get older, we assume they can manipulate numbers of complex ideas in their head. This can easily happen in Key Stage 2 where they still need 'props' for their learning, things like blocks for counting, or artefacts and films about days gone by. Those who have developmental learning problems will need props longer than the rest of the class. They may need counters, or coins, to help with their calculations, if they cannot do them in their head yet, and they may need pictures in their reading books to help them enjoy the stories. They may still need to play with art media, and need time to develop.

Much of the material defined in programmes of study is based on understanding at what age and stage children will best understand certain concepts. This is particularly true of subjects like science and geography, where understanding is so important to be able to move on to the next stage.

Using social constructivist theories

Through the work of Vygotsky, Chomsky and Bruner the importance of social contact and speech in learning is apparent; this means that group work, adult intervention and scaffolding are vital to learning. However, direct instruction, reading certain texts or following computer programs are not sufficient to enable pupils to reach their potential. These aids are clearly important, but brains are not just empty sponges waiting for the right liquid so they can expand and function; getting the balance right between intervention and encouraging independence is one of the most important skills you will have learnt when working with individual pupils. Similarly, the skills you have developed, when working with small groups in a class with the teacher taking the lead, will have given you an insight into how groups work. It is about sensing when the pupil or pupils have reached that 'zone of proximal development' and understanding what kinds of 'nudge' it needs to help them make the leap of understanding.

This means you also need to understand and engage with the social and cultural world in which your pupils are living and working.

> You do not have to become 'one of them', but learn about pupils' background, their motivations and interests and build on them.
> Share your background to create trust.
> What and who are their support mechanisms and relationships?
> What were their early learning experiences?

Understanding nuances of language on both sides is clearly important.

Pupils find more active approaches more stimulating, as well as useful. Making a game of the spellings, working as a group or doing an investigation require the pupils to be active physically as well as mentally. Practical work also brings together many of the above strategies, while group work encourages verbalisation and exchange of ideas. Health and safety procedures must be observed, of course, and pupils need to be taught to use tools correctly and associated skills. Endless worksheets are no answer to group work.

Using all the intelligences and VAK learning

It is tempting to assume that if we can determine how best a pupil learns, which intelligence is dominant for their mode of working, you will be able to plan and prepare work that optimises learning for that pupil. However, you may need rather to work on the areas in which the pupils function less well, in order to develop pathways of thinking that are currently underdeveloped. For instance, pupils who are very artistic or physical will benefit from developing skills in those areas, succeeding and growing in those areas, but they will also need to read, write and count to access further knowledge in their preferred field and the adult world they are approaching.

You need to understand a pupil's interests and leanings and build on them, to help them become as rounded a person as possible [3.3.1]. There are also ways of working for individuals which help them use one way of thinking to access another. For example, talk with pupils about having music on while learning something off by heart, singing straight prose or lists of things if they are musical; get them reading books about football or wildlife if their interests run that way; help the loners work in a group and the 'socialites' work on their own without talking. It is important that you try various approaches; consider the needs of the subject, the pupil, the whole class or group, and the possibility of having to work within the policies and syllabi of the school. You will still be under the direction of a teacher, so discuss all these approaches with him or her if you want to make any significant changes.

> **Try recalling some recent learning experiences with groups of pupils that you have been involved with**
> Which teaching approach did you use? Why?
> Think of a few learning experiences you have watched.
> What teaching approach did the teacher use? Why?
> Consider whether the method was chosen because
>
> it has always been done that way;
> that's what it suggested in the book;
> it seemed to fit the purpose.
>
> When you next plan some work, consider the various approaches suggested by these theories to see if you need to change anything.

Metacognition

As you can see from the above, there are many factors which you can consider when deciding how to teach, and they are complex and shifting. One of the most powerful strategies which takes them all into account is the move to get the pupils to think about the strategies for themselves, get them thinking about their own thinking and learning. This is called metacognition. If we can recognise how we best learn, our style, we can build on that knowledge. We can also train ourselves to get better. It is partly about understanding the different intelligences, but it is also about all the other pieces of the learning jigsaw: when help is needed; whether there are emotional or physical things stopping the process; what kinds of tools, books or equipment will help do a task; what kind of words might help. Fisher (2004) is quite clear that children who are trained in metacognitive skills become more self-aware and more self-evaluative.

Pollard, quoting the work of Nisbet and Shucksmith (1986), has a checklist of classroom strategies for developing thinking about learning:

Asking questions	Establishing aims and parameters of a task, discovering audience, relating a task to previous work.
Planning	Deciding on tactics and time schedules, reduction of task into manageable components, identification of necessary skills.
Monitoring	Continuing attempts to match efforts, solutions and discoveries to initial purposes.
Checking	Preliminary assessment of performance and results.
Revising	Redrafting and setting revised goals.
Self-testing	Final self-assessment of results and performance on task.

(Pollard 2002)

Fisher (ibid.) also gives some useful questions for pupils to ask themselves:

Questions assessing awareness of learning

- What have you learnt?
- What did you find hard?
- What do you need to learn/do next?

Questions prompting thinking about thinking

- What kinds of thinking have you been doing?
- Has your thinking changed?
- Did anyone say/do something that influenced/changed your thinking?

Questions probing attitudes and feelings

- What do you like doing/learning?
- What do you feel good/not good about?
- What do you feel proud of?

Questions setting targets

- What do you need to do better?
- What would help you?
- What are your targets?

When teaching about thinking or the processes of learning there are recommendations to target small groups who will benefit and clearly identify appropriate times and opportunities. So this is something that must be led by a class teacher, defining groups and purposes. You could, however, ask any of the above questions at any appropriate time. Some schools have gone into this area in a big way, so that all teachers use this approach somewhere, and adapt it with particular emphases for their subject or group of pupils. Ask around and find out who may be interested among your staff, and develop your own ideas in this area.

Some practical examples

Shayer and Adey (1981) have been working on cognitive acceleration (CA) since the 1970s, first as science teachers with *Towards a Science of Science Teaching* (1981), and have test evidence that their strategies increase grades in examinations, data which convinces sceptics that their ideas have some value. They talk of six pillars of learning: 1. Schema theory (Piaget), 2. Concrete preparation (Piaget), 3. Cognitive conflict (Vygotsky), 4. Social construction (Vygotsky), 5. Metacognition and 6. Bridging. Bridging aims to ensure that learning gained is generalisable, useful in circumstances in addition to those where that learning took place. Their recent book, *Learning Intelligence*, gives examples of cognitive acceleration in practice in classes from year 1 to year 9, in science education (CASE), mathematics education (CAME) and technology education (CATE) (Shayer and Adey 2002). The teacher concentrates on pedagogy, the way in which he or she presents the lesson, and Aday and Shayer believe that the three-piece model of lessons, or three Acts as they call it, supports a CA way of learning. It includes 'seeding questions' in the introduction, problem solving and discussion in the group work and whole-class discussion in the plenary. Metacognitive questions may arise at any time. Teachers can see the hierarchy both in the curriculum planning and in the different learning levels and intellectual development of the pupils. They can see the long-term aim of the series of lessons, the depth and breadth of the subject, contributing to the pupils' general education.

Some of you may have come across the work of de Bono (1971; 1972) who has been advocating divergent and creative thinking activities for many years, but they are not evaluated in the same way as the CASE materials. He suggests all kinds of thinking tools, such as thinking hats, and he has made lecturing and creating games his life's work and has a large website which you can tap into.

MacGilchrist and Buttress describe the learning journeys of a group of five schools in the London Borough of Redbridge. They believe their strategies supported and enhanced the learning capacity of children, teachers and the whole school. They were committed to inclusive education; a rich broad curriculum; and developing young people's confidence, self-esteem, and the skills and attitudes to help them become lifelong learners. The staff studied the literature around the various theories of learning in in-service sessions, inter-school visiting, contacts with the LEA and a local higher education institution and the development of critical friendship networks. They incorporated self-evaluation into their programme and developed a 'we can if . . .' attitude. Their conclusions emphasised the affective side of learning as well as the more technical aspects of the CA approach. They identified nine key principles in transforming their teaching and learning:

- a 'can do' culture;

- transformational leadership and management;

- the learning environment;

- ensuring a broad and balanced curriculum informed by assessment;

- enabling children to have a greater say in their learning and the management of the school;

- taking emotional intelligence seriously;

- assessment for learning;

- strengthening the learning dialogue between children, teachers and their parents;

- learning from the 'irritations' between summative and formative assessment.

(MacGilchrist and Buttress 2005)

Pick and choose

In practice you need to consider all these strategies, thus providing the learning environment that will support the pupils physically, emotionally, socially, culturally and spiritually. You should consider all the various cognitive theories and decide on the best fit, but you also need to consider whether the pupils can use what is being learnt. You can recognise from your own experiences that learning is built up from lots of little pieces and those flashes of insight are just from seeing the whole jigsaw picture from time to time. This, then, is an area in which to be interested and a lifelong learner yourself, and you should recognise there are no easy answers or short cuts; just keep watching, listening and learning yourself about learning.

To help assist learning you can:
- try to understand more about your own learning styles
- provide opportunities for repetition and reinforcement, vocabulary and scaffolding
- learn more about the social, cultural or emotional context in which the pupils are operating
- find out more about the individual needs of the pupils with whom you are working closely
- find out what experiences the learners have already had or what they might have missed
- learn something of the subjects they are learning for yourself, so that you know what might be coming next, or know what an appropriate strategy for that subject might be
- notice what kind of learning styles pupils have and talk with them about their own learning
- value pupils and their learning, appreciate what individuals have achieved and tell them – boost their self esteem
- be authentic and open, with pupils and adults
- ensure you know what is the learning intention of the teacher
- assist in creating a positive learning environment, both in the material surroundings and in attitudes to work and each other

- be part of the learning organisation that is your school, share your ideas and listen to others
- apply your learning to the situation in which you find yourself

Have high expectations of the pupils, yourself and learning standards.

(Watkinson 2002: 44)

Essential reading

One or more of these three:

Fox, G. (2001) *Supporting Children with Behaviour Difficulties*. London: David Fulton Publishers, pp. 19–31.

Hook, P. and Vass, A. (2000) *Creating Winning Classrooms*. London: David Fulton Publishers, pp. 22–38.

Watkinson, A. (2003b) *The Essential Guide for Experienced Teaching Assistants: Meeting the National Occupational Standards at Level 3*. London: David Fulton Publishers, pp. 74–5.

Some further reading

DfES (2004b) *Creating a Learning Culture: Conditions for Learning*. London: Department for Education and Skills, pp. 56–9, part of the Primary Strategy CPD materials. (References are given to supporting video and CD-ROM examples.)

Kyriacou, C. (1998) *Essential Teaching Skills* (2nd edn). Cheltenham: Nelson Thornes Ltd, Chapter 5, pp. 64–78.

Lang, P. (2004) 'Pastoral care and the role of the tutor', in V. Brooks, I. Abbott and L. Bills (eds) *Preparing to Teach in Secondary Schools*. Maidenhead and New York: Open University Press and McGraw-Hill Education, pp. 295–305.

Pollard, A. (2002) *Reflective Teaching: Effective and Evidence-informed Professional Practice*. London and New York: Continuum (especially Chapter 15 on social inclusion, pp. 356–9).

Titman, W. (1994) *Special Places: Special People – The Hidden Curriculum of School Grounds*. Godalming: World Wildlife Trust and Learning Through Landscapes (a well-illustrated and readable account).

Useful websites

Just type 'healthy schools uk' into your search engine to find out about your local activities. Try looking for any references to Edward de Bono.

www.ncaction.org/creativity is the government website supporting creative work.

CHAPTER 6

Context of learning: the curriculum and pupil behaviour

There was a lot mentioned in the last chapter about the learning environment and how this helps pupils to learn, but you will not be able to start from scratch. You will be working in someone else's classroom or laboratory with pupils for whom you are not ultimately responsible. You are neither their class teacher nor their parent or carer, so whatever you do will be set in a context which is not totally under your control. Teachers sometimes say, 'I could teach such and such a group or class if only their behaviour were better' as though poor behaviour is totally responsible for the lack of learning going on in the class. This is particularly felt about low level disruptive behaviour over which teachers can spend a lot of time and energy. Often it is just a few members of the class which cause the trouble; most pupils just seem to accept their lot and do what they are told. Discipline is a word often used in the negative sense meaning dealing with poor behaviour but properly used it should cover the positive as well as the negative aspects of behaviour.

Reread the Elton Report. It may be 'old' by some standards but it contains a great deal of useful information and tips which are still very relevant. For instance, their comment 'We are surprised to find that some schools are not following what seemed to us to be obvious good practice in simple matters' still holds (Elton 1989: 8).

There is increasing concern across the country about the level of poor behaviour in schools that is violent and very disruptive. The media coverage of the worst incidents, as with the reporting of any violent activity in society, tends to slew our perception of what actually goes on, leading us to believe that these kinds of incidents are regular occurrences. They are increasing, but are still thankfully rare. It is true that the general level of behaviour both in school and in the street is louder, more self-centred and more prone to violence than years ago, and pupils are less biddable, less responsive to authority. Peer pressure tends to encourage the extrovert. Concern is voiced about parenting, teachers are asking for behaviour management training and pupil referral units (PRUs) are seen as the only way to manage the few major disrupters, to allow the majority to work in a quieter environment more conducive to learning. Dealing with behavioural issues is high on the agenda of the teacher union conferences.

There are some ways of managing unwanted behaviour, and most of them are very simple [2.9]. It is important to distinguish between the low level minor annoying disruptions and the serious misdemeanours that need dealing with fairly and consistently according to the school's behaviour policy. The most important and useful way to deal with problems is to prevent them. Elton's evidence showed a broad measure of agreement that three factors were important in maintaining good classroom discipline: 'a teacher's competence has a strong influence on his or her pupils' behaviour . . . Knowledge of the subject to be taught is obviously crucial. [. . .] So is the ability to plan and deliver a lesson which flows smoothly and holds the pupils' attention. [. . .] The third area of competence comprises a range of skills associated with managing groups of pupils' (ibid.: 67).

Competence and confidence

If you are undertaking the short route to HLTA status then the school clearly feels you are already competent, and you feel confident to proceed without further training. The three days' 'briefing' is only an introduction to completing the paperwork and procedures to have your competence recognised. You will have been left on your own with a whole class as well as groups and individuals, and you will have coped well. As a recognised HLTA you will have a status within the school which is legally recognised as being able to maintain discipline. It should also mean you have both the job description and the role within the school that makes sure the pupils see you as their teacher for the time you are with them. This should immediately give you an inward sense of security that you can do the job. The rest is performance; your manner of assertion rather than aggression, your stance and demeanour, looking pupils in the eye and giving out an aura of authority.

Competence indicated is also needed in curriculum subject knowledge, not an area that this book can deal with in any detail [2.1]. If you want to hold your own in a class full of enquiring minds, or inspire those who see school as a penance, you need to be at least one step ahead of the class you are taking. This is not just a matter of reading the scheme of work (SOW) for the next week; it is about knowledge and understanding at a personal level, and about having a personal enthusiasm for the subject which you can transmit to the pupils [2.1].

Consider:
getting a copy of the school textbook for the area;
trying the school or local library for books on the particular part of the curriculum which you are going to teach;
talking to the subject co-ordinator or the head of department about where useful source material can be found, or what books or magazines he or she might recommend;
trying the book lists of the subject associations, looking out for their local meetings or conferences;
seeing if there is a local association which has meetings which you could attend, e.g. local history;
finding a course at a local college in the subject;
thinking about how your own interests might be linked with the subject, e.g. map reading when on holiday, natural history if you are a walker, mechanics if you maintain your own car or physical skills if you play any sport.

Photograph 6.1   The HLTA taking part of a history lesson while the teacher stands back

Photograph 6.2   The teacher takes over again

If you are dealing with disturbed children, which many of you may be, it is important that you have additional training. In-house training alongside the teachers on the details of the behaviour management policy is very valuable, but it does not mean that you need sophisticated strategies. Special training may include restraint procedures or counselling techniques. Again, neither of these can be dealt with in this book, as both require face-to-face training from specialists. All matters of behaviour management should conform to the policy of the school and, essentially, provide a consistent approach with the class teachers with whom you are working [3.3.4]. Ideally, behaviour management training should be done under a whole-school approach, with teachers and TAs getting the same training, so the approach throughout the school is consistent, pupils know that what any adult says goes and there are no easy rides or loopholes to slip through.

The importance of the curriculum

There have been times when I have observed classes where I am surprised the pupils, particularly the older ones, do not get up and walk out, the lessons are so boring! As an observer, I am bored; I cannot see the point of the lesson as it was not explained, the activity is repetitive and aimless. The teacher gets frustrated as little is achieved, and the pupils leave the room with an understanding that school, and that means any learning institution, is a boring place, to be disregarded in 'real' life; to be sat through if you are law abiding, escaped from or disrupted if you are not. So, one of the important things to understand in behaviour management in class is how to make the set curriculum more interesting, and how to engage the pupils in what is going on. Motivating pupils to learn should be high on your agenda [3.3.1].

Those of you in primary schools may think the problem relates only to secondary pupils, but that is not the case. The exact definitions of the curriculum, the publication of SOWs by the Qualifications and Curriculum Authority, although only advisory, the introduction of the Literacy and Numeracy Hours, have straitjacketed teachers' thinking. Even pre-schools have developed a formal curriculum, some insisting that young children, under-fives, sit and learn letters or how to count. No wonder that secondary schools have a truancy problem. The new Primary Strategy (DfES 2003c) has recognised the problem and its very title indicates the point I am trying to make: *Excellence and Enjoyment*. Making a set curriculum enjoyable is not necessarily easy, but surely more enjoyable for the teacher as well as the pupil. I can only point out some of the general principles to bear in mind when planning and preparing lessons here.

Prior to the NC, schools were free to decide what they taught. Although children mostly enjoyed school and schools were satisfied when saying their main aim was to be a happy place, schools, teachers and pupils slipped through the net. Either things like the tedious but necessary learning of spellings and tables went out of the window, or great chunks of subject knowledge were ignored. Now with the NC, greater accountability and the strategies in place ensure this will not happen, but it is also essential that the interest, enjoyment, meaning and purpose of learning are present in lessons. Given freedom, though, enabled schools and teachers to experiment: the sorts of things that happened were sometimes ephemeral, sometimes they resulted in lazy planning, but some excellent ideas came out. It is worth reflecting on some of these despite the fact that many teachers who trained in the last 20 years will not have used them or heard of them. However, the principles on which they were based still hold. Many of the ideas came from funded projects and resulted in considerable resources which may still be around mouldering in cupboards. Somehow, one needs to match the ideas from the projects with the structure of the NC.

Planning resources to extend meaning

Unless children have the experience of reading and writing for real, all the strategies in the world are not going to make them readers and writers. At one point we had a 'real books' project, the theory being that if you wanted children to read, by exposing them to real books, stories, picture books, factual books, whatever, they would want to decode them and thus learn to read. Where schools retained a mixed approach and a structure of graded but interesting readers, children thrived. Usually, one system predominated, for example phonics, 'look and say' with flashcards, or 'Breakthrough', where children wrote as they learnt words, or even the initial teaching alphabet (ITA), which depended on a special phonic alphabet of 40 letters. Lots of reading books supplemented the methods, and storytelling, story writing and drama all went together. Unsuccessful pupils were soon picked up and an alternative method would be tried, and special support sorted out. However, such a flexible but sensitive system needed considerable organisation, recording systems, resources and alert teachers to make it work. With lack of accountability, little inspection and variable to non-existent amounts of testing, standards varied widely across even local areas, let alone the country. Again, given appropriate funding for the books, and the appropriate organisation, there can be 'real books' and the Literacy Hour to put a structure to the teaching.

> **Think of the lessons where you have been present**
> What resources did you use?
> Were they worksheets and card games?
> Or were they artefacts associated with the subject area?
> Were the examples mentioned from real life or not?
> What use might the lesson have been to the pupils outside the classroom?
> Did you go outside the classroom at all while studying that subject?

Visits, visitors and artefacts

Teachers have been frightened off taking pupils out of school, even out of the classroom into the grounds in case there is an accident. This trend has been influenced by a few high profile cases, some sadly with tragic consequences. However, there are now extremely thorough guidelines available from government, LEAs and within schools which, if they are properly followed, should quell those fears. The day out of school should not merely have value as a 'day off', 'the annual 'trip' or an opportunity to socialise under different circumstances; it should be an integral part of the teaching to ensure that the relevance of the in-school lessons is made clear to the pupils [3.1.4].

> **When planning always think wider than the lesson**
> Where could you go?
> Who could come and talk?
> What video/DVD might illustrate the reality *well*, and not be a time filler?
> What objects or photographs would support the ideas of the lesson?
> Do any of the pupils have any ideas of what links could be made?
> When did the pupils last cook, make something useful, go in the grounds with their eyes open?
> When did they last debate issues arising from the subject of study?
> When did they last write for a specific purpose? E.g. a thank you letter, a story for a younger child, instructions.

Topic teaching

In the past, some primary schools developed a 'topic approach', with the whole curriculum planned around a centre of interest, including in extreme cases all the mathematics and English. In science, a major project was undertaken with children aged 5 to 13, where the topics were so general that all kinds of language, mathematics, history and geography could evolve from them. Subjects as vague as 'Holes, gaps and cavities' or as specific as 'Metals' could form the foundation for a whole term's work, and topic guides were produced for teachers and recording proforma developed. The whole project was care fully monitored and researched. Wynne Harlen's famous books *Match and Mismatch* recorded the findings and made suggestions for future work (Harlen *et al.* 1977a; 1977b).

At the time, while schools enjoyed the topics in the 5–13 series, the suggested monitoring of children's progress was considered too time consuming and cumbersome to be used systematically and the later recording of science NC which followed its introduction made Harlen's systems look simple by contrast. Her assessment ideas formed the foundation for the early science Standard Assessment Tasks (SATs) for seven-year-olds, which, being practical, also proved too time consuming. The strength of the recording system proposed also lay in the fact that things like attitude were recorded, and many skills were cross-curricular. Attitudes are rarely recorded systematically today. The content of the 5–13 books, if you can find any of these publications in your school, may still be useful to you when planning science activities for this age group.

Secondary schools, with an examination system to plan for and clear subject boundaries in their organisation, have always been more formal in their curriculum planning. Syllabuses were developed with weekly expectations of teaching matter regardless of pupil needs. Again, in science, there was a recognition that interest and reality had a major role in curriculum planning. The Science and Technology in Society (SATIS) project, heavily funded by industry, produced a vast amount of materials to support teachers and was highly thought of in the way in which pupils and teachers were motivated. Look around your schools and see if you can find any of this material. Some of the data may have dated, for example the statistics on transport, but the ideas for planning, activities and investigations are still valid. The first sets were published for pupils aged 14 to 19, then for pupils aged 8 to 14, and there is still some early years material available from ASE. *SATIS Across Europe* and *SATIS Across the World* are still in use and involve schools exchanging information on scientific areas such as food or transport, thus adding yet another dimension to the pupils' interest in the world around them.

You may say that all the above is irrelevant, that we live in the twenty-first century and topics are a thing of the past, that the materials mentioned above are out of date, and do not relate to the NC. This is only partly true. If some of the ideas from those topics were incorporated now but in a limited way, developing themes, topics with only a few relevant subjects involved, then it is possible to have the best of both worlds: structure and interest. There is still a place for thematic approaches to provide coherence. Cohen *et al.* (2004) have some topic planning formats in their chapter on planning.

Thinking across the subject boundaries

Unless the pupils can see a reason for what they are learning, it is merely a time occupying exercise, to be got through until the next break. Some pupils like learning for its own sake, mopping up facts like sponges, but they will be the minority; most, given a reason and a long-term goal, will be prepared to do the necessary rote learning to realise that goal. However, there is evidence that Years 5 and 6 children who can form complex sentences for their Literacy Hour cannot write imaginatively or creatively; the flow of language once so lauded in the pre-NC schools appears lost. Mathematical ideas developed in the Numeracy Hour, like making or reading graphs, are not always used in the science lessons, or certainly not at the same time to provide the relevance and coherence which would help. This problem becomes even more acute in secondary schools, where subject teachers isolate themselves in areas and plan and deliver their syllabi away from other subject colleagues. At least in most primary schools, the class teacher knows which parts of each curriculum have been covered by a particular time and can revise skills in one area that may be showing as weaknesses in another.

An example of cross-curricular work

A mixed Year 3/Year 4 class were due to include story writing in the Literacy Hour, including the idea of chapters. The teacher, when planning this, considered how to make the story relevant and introduced the idea of writing a story for the Reception class. As young children like pop-up books and books with pages they can feel, she realised that here was a link with the design and technology (DT) SOW for her age group, so she altered the timing of the plans from that indicated on the original long-term plans to coincide. During the half-term the children learnt about stories and audience, as well as making two-dimensional moving parts. Towards the end of term she timetabled some whole afternoons to make a story book with moving and feeling pages, and with the help of a TA, she also included some ICT. The children had planned their stories in groups on prepared planning sheets, with outlines of the pictures and notes about the texts for each chapter. Then, in the long sessions the stories were written in sections on word processors, to be cut and pasted on the pages being constructed by others in the groups. The teacher arranged for fabric and card resources to be available, with appropriate glue. When observed, the whole class were on task, absorbed, interested and ready to explain to anyone interested exactly what they had done, why and how they had done it, who was involved and what would happen next.

It seems fairly obvious that English or literacy is needed in every subject as speaking and listening make up the major part of any lesson. Reading and writing are the accepted forms, of communication for class work and homework, but mathematics, or numeracy, is as important but not always recognised so clearly. The KS3 mathematics framework encourages teachers to do just this kind of thing – collect data from geography field trips, take examples from science lessons. It also encourages non-mathematics teachers to recognise the use of mathematics ideas in their lessons. If you are working in secondary schools see if you can find any of the cross-curricular materials which came into schools in 2001/2002 on teaching mathematics across the curriculum. There is an assumption that pupils need mathematics to level 4 NC, that reached by an average Year 6 pupil, to access the secondary curriculum. This should give you an added impetus to make sure you get the level 2 qualification on the National Qualifications Framework through the Learning and Skills Council provision, whether or not you are going for the HLTA status. You will then be able to assist in any lesson when mathematical ideas occur.

In planning
Consider (easier in primary schools):

books of interest in a history or science topic to be used in literacy;
the teaching of different graphs in mathematics to coincide with the need to use them in science;
sources of food in geography and refer to it in RE when talking of the customs of different faiths;
using as many real examples as possible;
showing how tables learnt are used in shopping (how to shop without a calculator and make sure you are not conned!);
recognition of punctuation or spellings learnt as they appear in writing in history or PSHE.

The Primary Strategy is pointing the way for this approach. Pages 35 and 36 of the booklet entitled *Designing Opportunities for Learning* gives two lesson plans, one with separate lessons unlinked, the second where the ideas are linked between the lessons (DfES 2004c).

Subject weeks

Some schools still have subject orientated weeks; again, it is easier to plan in primary schools.

An example of cross-curricular topic week from a subject week

The teacher of a mixed Year 5 and 6 class planned a technology week without reference to an NC SOW. She asked the pupils to pair up with a friend and bring a cardboard carton into school about 30 to 50 cm long, wide and deep. The task was to make it into a stage with at least one working part and one use of an electric circuit. The results were some completely written stage scripts, miniature sets with characters who moved, or scenery that changed, stage lighting or special effects and final presentations that were videoed. No exercise books were seen all week, no teacher-directed lessons took place except PE. The biggest problem was how to evaluate the children's work in NC terms. The enthusiasm, commitment, enjoyment, problem solving, discussion were only too obvious, and the end results were very satisfying to all the children, who were immensely proud to show off their productions to visitors. The two DT teachers from local secondary schools were very impressed and almost humbled by the children's expertise and confidence.

While the end result was not directly transferable to a test situation or marks on an assessment grid, the children had seen the usefulness of the skills they had learnt in more formal lessons and had a great sense of achievement. Sometimes such weeks can take place after the SATs when the pressure is off. Another type of activity which can have similar results is to plan a performance for the end of the year, for which the pupils have to write the script, paint and make the scenery and costumes, write invitations and organise seating and tickets. Entertaining a community group, with planning and making food and entertainment is another suggestion. When planning with a teacher or teachers, make suggestions and especially indicate how you can help.

Other ways of increasing curriculum relevance

While finding out what interests the pupils, you must also keep hold of your values and that of the school; you should not pander to the interests of a dominant few. Try to avoid any political, religious, ethnic or gender bias in your choices, or make sure you balance one session with ones giving differing points of view.

Consider the pupils' perspectives – what makes things come alive for them?
Always try to introduce an element of challenge in any work you set.
Discuss the marking policy carefully with each of the teachers you work with. A majority of parents and 'the public' still believe that any piece of written work should be total marked for all spelling and punctuation mistakes regardless of the purpose of the writing, be it for notes, creativity or recording an experiment.
Consider the best way of recording anything:

photocopy a scribe's record for group work;
use a digital camera for an investigation and reproduce the result.

Use drama, films, artefacts, games.
Don't rely on the ubiquitous worksheet however well designed or amenable to 'colouring in'.
Keep the aim of the lesson clear to the pupils, at both the beginning and the end.

None of this detracts from the discipline of a subject. It is a matter of understanding and getting round the problems of organisation and resourcing, and the tracking of children's progress. The secret lies in the planning, more of which in the next chapter. It is here you can brainstorm your ideas and discuss their feasibility. Elton recommended that 'all parties involved in planning, delivery and evaluation of the curriculum should recognise that the quality of its content and the teaching and learning methods through which it is delivered are important influences on pupils' behaviour' (Elton 1989: 104).

It must also be remembered that the informal and hidden curriculum operating outside the classroom is part and parcel of a pupil's school experience. Consistent behaviour management strategies in place outside the classroom and the care of the environment will induce respect, affecting the way in which your classroom strategies work. If a teacher ignores certain behaviour in the corridor, perhaps because it is during breaktime, the pupils may immediately think they can get away with things with that person. As an assistant it is particularly important that you are seen both inside and outside the classroom as carrying adult, school supported, authority. This does not mean being arrogant, stand-offish or officious. The friendly approach is a positive one, which only becomes unfriendly if necessary.

Behaviour management

There has been a great deal written and spoken about how to deal with poor behaviour. If you have planned an interesting lesson and prepared the materials beforehand and remember things like confidence and 'presence', you should have fewer problems with behaviour. You are avoiding the 'boring' lesson, where any activity is preferable to doing the task set. Kyriacou (1998) lists boredom in what he sees as the main causes of misbehaviour; however, he also includes prolonged mental effort, inability to do the work, being sociable, low academic self-esteem, emotional difficulties, poor attitudes and lack of negative consequences. So, there are other things which can help when planning and preparing lessons.

As a TA in the school, you will have worked there with individual and groups of pupils. This means you are likely to know the pupils well. This also means you know the kind of pace at which they can work and you are prepared for the kinds of emotional difficulties they might have; you will understand what attitudes they might have to the school or work, and why they have them. Most lessons where there is low level disturbance are actually the least challenging, slowest paced lessons, so again the boredom factor enters in. You will know which pupils have particularly low self-esteem or low self-confidence, and you have considered strategies for dealing with these. You most probably have worked with pupils who have difficulties with learning and so you know whether the class you are to take is capable of understanding what you have to teach. Many of you have been differentiating the teacher's worksheets, reinterpreting his or her instructions and supporting the lower ability groups for some time. No wonder many HLTAs are being used to take classes of the lower ability range.

Note the last point Kyriacou makes: lack of negative consequences. As an HLTA, left in charge of a class of pupils, you must be able to use as many of the strategies of behaviour management as possible that are available to a teaching member of that school, otherwise you will be seen as a soft option. Just ensure that you clarify the point at which you refer to a teacher or the senior management team in the case of serious misdemeanours with your mentor/line manager/class teacher. This may be at an earlier point in the consequences list than with a qualified teacher. For instance, if the usual consequence of refusal to carry out instructions is some kind of detention, it may be that you are not empowered to carry this out, but would have to send the pupil with a note to a particular member of staff to get such an action endorsed. You might feel the behaviour that occurred should prevent the pupil from going on a forthcoming trip, that he or she cannot be trusted on public transport. It is likely that such a prohibition would be the decision of the class teacher, not you, and you would be preventing the pupil taking part in a planned part of the curriculum. The class teacher must take responsibility for the learning opportunities of the pupils. A discussion beforehand might pre-empt any later problems, or complaints from parents.

Cohen's chapter on managing behaviour in the classroom is a very comprehensive account of the various strategies you can adopt (Cohen *et al.* 2004). Noticeably, they start with reference to the school values and behaviour policy framework. It is vital that you work within this [2.9, 3.3.4]; however, even within a school with a weak tradition of consistent approaches you can establish your personality with a classroom. The school may serve a catchment area where attitudes are anti anyone or anything in authority, where arguments are more common than discussions, where violence is an answer to problems and aggression is a sign of strength, but your approach is what matters when you are in charge. An important factor is consistency of approach whatever the incident. Some of the policies that do not directly give guidance about behaviour management are also important in this area. For instance, if you withdraw a pupil from class because he or she is behaving badly you are depriving him or her of that part of the curriculum, but sometimes it has to be done; restraining a pupil could be construed as child abuse; dealing with bullying may be in a separate policy. You must know the limits of your authority, and when and to whom you should refer incidents outside that authority. Good communication systems need to be in place before you are left on your own.

Cohen *et al.* also point out that in addition to ensuring interesting curriculum content, matching the work to the pupils and understanding relationships, classroom organisation, resource provision and teaching and learning styles can influence how behaviour evolves. Discipline is positive and needs to be thought about before the lesson, and is not something to be evoked when things go wrong. Prevention, being proactive and having positive approaches should be the key to a productive learning lesson. Attention to some of the ideas in the next chapters should help in planning and performance, and strategies such as having all the resources you need and giving instructions clearly all add to a style that will reduce problems [3.3.8].

There are various tips and strategies for dealing with disturbances if they do occur; these ideas are all helpful and most are common sense. Elton lists the main features of good practice in dealing with such behaviour found in a search of the literature.

Teachers should:

27.1   know the pupils as individuals. This means knowing their names, their
           personalities and interests and who their friends are;

27.2 plan and organise both the classroom and the lesson to keep pupils interested and minimise the opportunities for disruption. This requires attention to basics such as furniture layout, grouping of pupils, matching work to pupils' abilities, pacing the lessons well, being enthusiastic and using humour to create a positive classroom atmosphere;

27.3 be flexible in order to take advantage of unexpected events rather than being thrown off balance by them. Examples would include the arrival of the window cleaner or a wasp in the middle of a lesson;

27.4 continually observe or 'scan' the behaviour of the class;

27.5 be aware of and control their own behaviour, including stance and tone of voice;

27.6 model the standards of courtesy that they expect from pupils;

27.7 emphasise the positive, including praise for good behaviour as well as good work;

27.8 make the rules for classroom behaviour clear to the pupils from the first lesson and explain why they are necessary;

27.9 make sparing use of reprimands. This means being firm rather than aggressive, targeting the right pupils, criticising the behaviour not the person, using private rather than public reprimands where possible, being fair and consistent, and avoiding sarcasm and idle threats;

27.10 make sparing and consistent use of punishments. This includes avoiding the group punishment which pupils see as unfair. It means avoiding punishments which humiliate pupils by, for example, making them look ridiculous. This breeds resentment; and

27.11 analyse their own classroom management performance and learn from it. This is the most important message of all.

(Elton 1989: 71,72)

Pollard (2002) talks of the flow of lessons. Each part has a shape; beginning, middle and end, and a lesson has pace; it wants to flow at the appropriate pace for the pupils to keep their interest yet allow them thinking time. He recognises transitions between sections of the lessons as possible danger points for diversionary tactics. You should be on the lookout for this; for example, observe how teachers manage their transitions. At any time there can be a crisis, brought about by things beyond your control: some pupil knocking into another pupil or an inadvertent comment badly received by a pupil who 'got out of bed the wrong side'. Keeping an eye out for potential flare points in the lesson will help you deal with such situations, but thinking through the composition of characters before a lesson can also help.

Negative behaviour may be verbally or physically abusive or offensive, racial or sexist actions or language should not be tolerated, and bullying needs to be recognised and dealt with [3.3.7]. You must also recognise that sometimes circumstances change, for both pupils and the school, and be alert to these changes. Changing rooms or buildings or going from inside the school to the playground or sports field can alter behaviour.

We all need boundaries so rules are developed. We all have rights, but we also have responsibilities, which includes access to school facilities, equipment and materials for staff and pupils, and developing responsibility in pupils. The aim is to make pupils take responsibility for their own behaviour. The behaviour management training (DfEE 2000) talks of the 4Rs approach: Rules, Routines, Rights and Responsibilities leading to choices which have consequences. Hayes (2000) suggests a 7Rs approach. He does not include Rights, and suggests that Rooms, Relationships, Roles and Realities all have a part to play in establishing and managing effective control on the classroom.

The language of choice is powerful: say to a pupil who might argue with you 'you have a choice – you can do what you know is right or . . .' Whatever the consequence is for that misbehaviour, it will affect your school.

Using the language of choice

- It gives children confidence by giving them responsibility
- It regards mistakes as a normal part of learning
- It removes the struggle for power
- It has a positive emphasis
- It is an overt link between principles and strategy.

(DfEE 2000: 17)

Your school may have a systematic reward system, with stickers and certificates for achievements, and there may also be a sanctions or punishment system. In the classroom, you are on the spot to see to the immediate situation, and you will have established what punishments you are able to use.

Where possible you should deal with matters immediately upon seeing inappropriate behaviour [3.3.7]. The secret is to be assertive without being aggressive or confrontational and to ensure that you are separating any views you have on inappropriate behaviour from your views on the pupil. This enables the pupil to save face and maintain his or her self-esteem, which is probably low. Keep the focus on the primary behaviour, the thing that drew your attention in the first place and actively try to build up your relationship with the pupil concerned. Always follow up on things that count: if you have said you will refer the matter to someone else, or you will talk to him or her again on the next day, then be sure you do it. Always seek help if you need it. If you see a potential problem situation, make someone else aware, and attempt to defuse it. Ensure you have a message system to communicate with a more senior member of staff. Such a situation can occur with an individual if there is shortage of equipment, or a challenging piece of work; or with a group, for instance, in a slow queue forming to use a special piece of equipment. Typical positive strategies include appropriate praise and encouragement. Pupils who are motivated and interested are less likely to misbehave. Do not touch or restrain a pupil in a conflict situation unless you have been specially taught the procedure for your school.

Kyriacou has written some useful ideas on the use of punishments. He suggests their purpose is for retribution, deterrence and rehabilitation, usually a combination of all three. He also points out that the very use of punishments recognises that other strategies have been unsuccessful. Punishments have drawbacks:

They form an inappropriate model for human relationships.

They foster anxiety and resentment.

They have a short lived 'initial shock' effect.

They encourage pupils to develop strategies to avoid getting caught.

They do not promote good behaviour directly but simply serve to suppress misbehaviour.

They focus attention on the misbehaviour.

(Kyriacou 1998: 93)

An example of the positive use of lack of punishment

The school fire alarm sounded in a large secondary school. The school was evacuated and all the appropriate checks carried out. No smoke or fire was found and so a misdemeanour was suspected. No culprit was immediately evident. An hour later, at breaktime, two girls appeared at the deputy head's door. One was in tears. Her friend told the deputy that the one in tears believed she had inadvertently set the alarm off with her elbow. The deputy managed to calm the girl sufficiently to get her to tell what happened. She was clearly anxious about what would happen to her on owning up, but had felt the school systems were sufficiently fair that her story would be believed. The deputy did accept her story; he knew which fire point had been activated and it coincided with the girl's story. He felt that while she had caused a big nuisance to everyone in the school and created a false alarm, she recognised what she had done was silly. She had obviously been larking about and she had had the courage to own up. He also realised that she was already very upset. She was not punished, but sent back to class with a 'thank you for telling me'. Clearly the culture in the school enabled her to own up in the first place, and this was reinforced by the fairness with which she was treated.

Kyriacou suggests the following negative consequences – or punishments – could be considered:

Writing tasks – maybe this is the problem,

Detention – needs permission,

Loss of privileges – need to have them in the first place,

Exclusion from the class – but who will supervise?

Verbal intimidation – a telling off should take place in private,

Informing significant others – may be your only option, but may be misconstrued by the pupil,

Symbolic punishment – recording somewhere to accumulate,

Exclusion from school – not within your power.

You can quickly see that they all have their disadvantages. Their effective use also depends on the following:

Sparing use

Timing

Tone of voice and body language
Fitting the punishment to the crime
Due process – fairness
Relationship to school policy
Aversiveness – unpleasantness for the pupil.

You need to find out:

what is appropriate for:

- classrooms
- different teachers' classrooms (will vary slightly)
- within other areas of the school
- outside the school premises even. Laboratories or technical areas will have different rules or codes of practice
- individuals
- groups
- whole classes

what are:
the rules
the rewards and sanctions that can be applied

by you
by others

what strategies are available for you to use in managing inappropriate behaviour
time out places
sources of help and referral at different times of the day
report forms or notes
withdrawal of privileges

how you
report incidents
develop your skills of behaviour management
seek advice

(Watkinson 2003)

Essential reading

Your school's behaviour management policy

Elton, R. (1989) *Discipline in Schools* (Report of the Committee of Enquiry). London: Department of Education and the Welsh Office.

Fox, G. (1998) *A Handbook for Learning Support Assistants*. London: David Fulton Publishers (helpful for giving the rationale for some poor behaviour and includes simple strategies for group working).

Some further reading

Cohen, L., Manion, L. and Morrison, K. (2004) *A Guide to Teaching Practice* (5th edn). London: RoutledgeFalmer, Chapter 15, pp. 277–320 (very comprehensive).

DfES (2002a) *Self-study Materials for Supply Teachers: Classroom and Behaviour Management.* London: Department for Education and Skills, p. 97. (These self-study materials are available free from the DfES and have some very useful checklists. This booklet particularly has helpful practical suggestions for classroom practice.)

Hook, P. and Vass, A. (2000a) *Confident Classroom Leadership.* London: David Fulton Publishers.

Hook, P. and Vass, A. (2000b) *Creating Winning Classrooms.* London: David Fulton Publishers.

Kyriacou, C. (1998) *Essential Teaching Skills* (2nd edn). Cheltenham: Nelson Thornes Ltd, Chapter 6, pp. 79–101.

Pollard, A. (2002) *Reflective Teaching: Effective and Evidence-informed Professional Practice.* London and New York: Continuum, Chapter 11, pp. 239–58.

Rogers, B. (2000) *Classroom Behaviour.* London; Thousand Oaks, CA and New Delhi: Paul Chapman Publishing (Sage); Sage Publications Inc. and Sage Publications India Pvt Ltd. (A most useful readable aid to behaviour management.)

CHAPTER 7

Planning and preparation

Some TA/HLTAs that I have observed working to date, taking classes in classrooms on their own, appear to be working really as cover supervisors. The planning for the lesson has been the teacher's. They have helped in some of the ideas behind the planning, made resources for the lesson, but they have not been involved with the planning of that lesson; the teacher left his or her planning for the TA to carry out. TA/HLTA ownership of any planning or serious participation in planning appeared to be left to planning for small groups, where the teacher or manager had delegated certain responsibilities to the TA. An example would be the Additional Literacy support materials for classes working through the Literacy Hour. It could therefore be possible that some HLTAs will see this chapter as irrelevant; either they are just picking up the teacher's plans and working with them, or the materials, such as those provided for the Literacy Hour, are dictating the planning. The process of joint planning, the talking together that is so vital to a good teacher/TA or teacher/HLTA relationship, is essential for effective work in the classroom.

It is a vital part of an HLTA's role both to participate in the planning with the teacher(s) with whom they work and whose classes they might take, and to make some of their own plans or adaptations to the teachers' plans. This will ensure they both understand them and can evaluate what they have done. Using the teacher's plans alone is not sufficient. I am sure this statement will be contentious as heads and managers are not providing paid planning time for you when writing contracts. Any joint planning done seems still to depend on the goodwill of the assistant. You should have paid planning time, and this matter should be taken seriously both by you and by your managers. Your role is to add value to the learning opportunities for the pupils and by you cannot do this 'on a wing and prayer'. Standard 3.1.1 asks you to 'contribute effectively to the teacher's planning and preparation'. Effectiveness takes thought and consideration, communication and co-operation, all of which take time and must be valued appropriately.

The School Support Staff guidance notes for TAs were drawn up by the NJC (National Joint Council for Local Government Services made up of all the teacher unions, Unison, GMB, TGWU and the Employers' Organisation). These say that a level 4 TA would be able to 'within an agreed system of supervision, plan challenging teaching and learning objectives to evaluate and adjust lesson/work plans as appropriate' and produce 'lesson plans, worksheets, plans etc' (NJC 2003: 13). Good practice in giving the planning, preparation and assessment (PPA) time to teachers – the 10 per cent due to all of them in

September 2005 – also states 'support staff who undertake specified work, particularly those working to HLTA standards, should have paid time set aside to enable them to plan and prepare for their own role in lessons and liaise with their class teachers. Support staff planning and preparation should be within their contracted time but not necessarily within the timetable teaching day' (NRT 2004: 5).

While some of you may be just interpreting the teachers' plans rather than devising your own, the intention in this chapter is to work through the principles and processes of planning that the teacher will have gone through to give you, as an HLTA, an insight into what is going on. So, when you pick up a plan and are just interpreting the teacher's work, or you get to plan lessons or part of them for yourself, you will have some understanding of the underlying thinking. You should be able to contribute more and make someone else's plans come alive for the pupils. There is a very clear distinction between a cover supervisor and an HLTA; the latter should be able to advance the learning of the pupils. You will only be able to do this if you are actively involved in the planning process of the lesson, even mentally.

Why bother with plans at all? I am sure you have seen teachers, albeit rarely these days, go into a lesson seemingly without a plan. Many experienced teachers will say, if asked for a written plan, 'Well, I only do it in full when Ofsted are around'. So they apparently see plans as largely something required by someone else and not something of use to them. This is not really true. They are only able to go into a lesson without that particular lesson plan because of their experience. They have done a lot of longer-term planning, they know where the day fits into the proposals for the term and the year, carefully thought through by themselves and others. Their experience has internalised many of the everyday things that can occur in the lesson. It is more than likely that they have taught that lesson before and have even internalised the plans from a previous time. In other words, they have planned, but just not written it down in a formal way on that day. You do not have this experience to draw on. Also teachers, while training and early on in their careers, would have had to plan everything in writing, and now, for special occasions, they will still draw up detailed plans.

The other thing to remember is that the formal planning suggested by the strategies and the SOWs published by QCA came about because teachers had not always been planning in detail. Originally, the NC did not have to be covered, and then when it arrived, teachers were not trained in using it to plan. Some LEAs suggested SOWs and published them, which proved so useful in stopping teachers on a widespread basis from reinventing wheels that the nationally published ones became available. Then the strategies actually suggested formats for planning on paper. While helpful, these have become part of the straitjacketing identified in the new Primary Strategy. Various websites have ready-made plans for all sorts of subjects, occasions, ages and types of pupils. The only trouble with these is that unless the teacher personalises them for their circumstances, and really understands the various bits of them, they could result in a rather sterile and possibly irrelevant presentation for the pupils. It is all a question of balance, using resources like those available but ensuring that you make them your own. This is the point made at the beginning: you cannot make the best use of the teacher's planning unless you make them your own [2.2, 3.1.2].

The purpose of planning

There are many reasons why planning is necessary and important beyond any accountability to line managers or outside inspectors.

Consider any event in your family, for example an important birthday or anniversary
What kind of planning will you do? What lists do you make? What plans do you write down? Who do you involve?
What kind of event is it going to be? What timescale?
What about a timetable of events within the major event?
Who will be coming?
A guest list
What can you afford to spend?
Mini-spreadsheet for costings/back of an envelope
What food?
Caterers or self-catering
Recipes and timetable for preparations
What venue?
Research, booking
Entertainment, accommodation for guests, what to wear . . .
More research, lists and timetables.

I am not suggesting that each lesson needs this kind of planning; you could think of the above in relation to say a week's or a term's work – lots of lessons go to make up that, and lots of little bits go to make up the planning of the event.

Think. Why would you draw up plans for the event?
It could be:

to reduce your stress and anxiety;
to be able to share your ideas with others;
to give yourself time for research and find or prepare resources/furniture/equipment/ tools;
to give yourself confidence to deviate because you have thought things through;
to ensure you do think things through;
to consider the needs of the guests;
to consider all possible eventualities – weather, illness, safety;
to give you time to reflect on ideas and decisions;
to build up good relationships with anybody else involved in the process – guests or providers;
as an aide memoir when you panic;
to refer to next time you get involved in the same kind of thing;
to enable someone else to take over in a crisis.

School plans are useful for all of these purposes – just substitute pupils for guests and other staff for providers on the event planning above. You can also see how prior experiences, knowledge of resources, availability of experts, other people's/staff ideas, consulting the guests/pupils, access to other kinds of plans can all help the planning process. You can also see how knowing the organiser/teacher and the way he or she thinks and envisages the outcome, the purpose of the event and something about the guests/pupils are going to make all the difference if you have to take over organisation at a moment's notice. You can see why the school likes to employ you to take a class rather than a supply teacher that does not have that insider knowledge.

It is in planning that you can consider the environment and strategies mentioned in the last two chapters to ensure you provide an interesting context to learning using a variety of methods to aid the process for the maximum number of pupils. Kyriacou gives ten features of effective teaching which are very useful to consider when planning:

Teachers should make use of a variety of teaching methods.
There should be use of investigative, inquiry and problem-solving activities.
Learning activities should involve pupils communicating their ideas to others.
Use should be made of both independent work and collaborative small group work tasks.
Pupils should evaluate their own work and the work of others.
Use should be made of a variety of learning materials, such as books, videos and
information technology packages.
Use should be made of direct teaching methods, most importantly question and answer.
Learning should take place in different contexts, such as at home, in the community,
during fieldwork and in visits.
Pupil's work should be presented in a variety of ways.
Learning activities should help pupils to develop positive attitudes about the subject and
about themselves as learners, also desirable personal qualities such as perseverance.

(Kyriacou 1998: 145, 146)

Hopefully, metacognitive strategies and questions can be built into some or part of your lessons, so that the pupils are always improving the ways they learn how to learn.

Whole-school planning

Anything you do must fit into the school's way of working [2.3]. First, you must understand where in the scheme of things a lesson plan stands. Figure 7.1 gives you a diagrammatic version of how it all works.

The governors and teachers will review the aims of the school probably every three years or so and hopefully will involve all sections in the school community in drawing these up: support staff, parents, pupils and possibly even the wider community around the school. You should make sure you feed your views into such a process and encourage your support staff colleagues to do likewise. Teachers then plan each year to ensure continuity between years and coverage during the year. These are called long-term plans. They may use SOWs from websites, syllabi from examination boards, published textbook schemes as well as their own ideas. It is not likely that they will involve support staff in these decisions, but

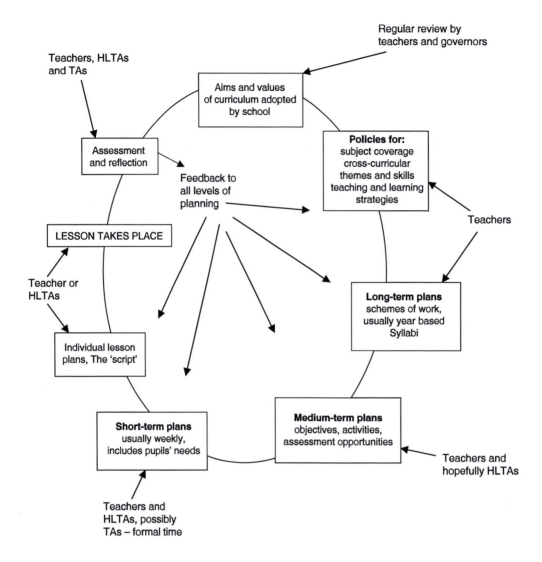

Figure 7.1   The whole-school planning cycle

you should have access to the plans they draw up. Since the introduction of the NC the links between primary and secondary should be better, but one rarely hears of schools exchanging their long-term plans to see if there is continuity between the two phases, or between first, middle and upper where this system exists. The more the school is able to make these plans their own and build in local interests and opportunities, the more likely they are to be matched to the local circumstances.

A long-term planning example

The teachers of a primary school serving an old fishing village with marshland and picturesque waterfront buildings wanted to ensure they used their surroundings when planning their curriculum. The school was large enough to have just one class per year group so the major schemes and NC plans matched their class structure fairly easily.

They then considered visits, outings and resources. They allocated a visit to the waterfront for each year group but with different objectives.

YR and Y1 would just be having a picnic sometime during the summer term. Surprisingly a survey of the children had shown that only about half of them ever went there. Alongside this would be walks to the local recreation ground, church and a few small group visits to some of the shops. The aim was to train the children to go out from school, making the village familiar from a school point of view – looking properly, talking about it, remembering places of interest.

Y2 were going to include some drawing activities of the old buildings.

Y3 were going to look at the various boats and associated activities.

Y4 were going to go out on the marshes on the paths to look at the various forms of wildlife – birds, saltwater plants, and so on.

Y5 were going to include a study of the church building, alongside the other buildings of interest in various places in the village.

Y6 were going to spend a day with the local wildlife expert down on the marshes, as a preliminary to a residential field trip later in the summer term. The field trip would include ancient buildings and wild areas.

The teachers drew up a similar plan for the use of the new wildlife area recently opened in the school grounds. Simply pond dipping each year would be repetitive and inefficient, so links were made with the science and geography schemes. They then realised that similar plans could be made for festivals so that Guy Fawkes did not recur in every class in the same way. They were linked with the art scheme so that wax resist occurred one year, use of oil pastels another and so on. This kind of planning needed tweaking as different staff brought different ideas: somebody found a boat builder willing to talk and take visits of groups, the local wildlife warden became involved. The local religious leaders became interested, and an exchange with a school in London was arranged to ensure a wider cultural coverage than would otherwise be available.

The teachers draw up the medium-term plans and may well involve you at this stage. Some TAs, long before the idea of HLTAs in primary schools, were often class based even though their job description or funding meant they should concentrate on one child. They spent time with the teachers in the holidays, especially the summer holidays, unpaid just going through the long-term plans for the term ahead. Involvement at this early stage meant they could offer ideas and really understand some of the teacher's intentions when the activities occurred [3.1.2]. Now there are HLTAs, they should be involved at this level (and paid for it) as this means the emergency taking over of a class or regular PPA time cover will be much more meaningful. This can only be to the benefit of the pupils.

Medium-term plans usually outline objectives in each curriculum area, associated activities, assessment opportunities and resources. It is at this stage that basic risk assessment should be done to ensure the proposals being made will be safe. Then resources can be obtained, booked, made or prepared. HLTAs are being used for resource provision particularly in secondary schools where bureaucracy seems to have dominated the teacher's timetable.

Short-term plans are often a weekly timetable with notes and maybe two to four lessons planned in detail. Learning intentions for the week are established here and consideration is given to the needs of the pupils, and it is here that grouping will be planned. Planning for different pupils does not usually start until the short-term plan stage. It is here that issues of differentiation will arise, IEP targets will need to be considered and the detailed timetable of the lesson considered. Sets and ability groups may be established on a termly basis, but their detailed planning will only take place on assessment of weekly progress. This kind of assessment, informing the planning ahead, is called formative assessment. It may be formal or informal, it may just be a matter of judging whether the group understood or needs a session to repeat the same material, or it may be a question of changing the sessions to accommodate progress. How IEP targets are incorporated will be a matter for the teacher to decide, but if you have responsibility for individual pupils in any way or are line managed by the SENCO it is likely you will have valuable insights into the best way to proceed.

The national strategies introduced some weekly planning sheets for use just with their subjects. While these have their uses particularly in the early days of unfamiliarity with the framework, this has resulted in some considerable over-planning with a high amount of detail, chunks of the strategy being cut and pasted, electronically or handwritten onto the format. If it takes five hours every weekend to plan just for literacy and numeracy using such formats, you can see why science and the foundation subjects have been neglected. It is not your role to be planning in this way, but you may well be given copies of the teacher's plans using this format to follow. Get the teacher concerned to explain which bits you need to take notice of and make sure you have copies of the relevant frameworks.

Subject planning

Much of the hard work has been taken out of this with the published SOWs based on the NC. However, what is not planned so well are those elements of the NC that sometimes get forgotten: breadth and balance and coherence. Progression and coverage are often considered to be largely addressed by the NC itself and the associated SOWs; however, the progression between year groups and more significantly between phases is less well addressed unless records and planning are really used together at the transition times for the pupils. Breadth and balance can be both between subjects and within the subject. This should be the concern of the teachers when doing their long-term and medium-term planning. Coherence is partly about the cross-curricular links mentioned in the last chapter, but more about making the learning meaningful. It is about how the pupils actually receive and experience what is going on in a lesson. It is salutary from time to time to explore this with the pupils; ask them what they actually think about having certain lessons or tasks.

Pupil needs' planning

The Code of Practice clearly sets out the procedures for identification, assessment and provision for pupils with SEN. The stages School Action, School Action Plus and Statements cover school responses to pupils with SEN. You also know that there are pupils, not so labelled, who need extra help in some areas or from time to time. The teacher may or may not group these children for some activities. If there is grouping you need to know its rationale and the membership of the groups. Your school may even have setting or even lower ability streams, where all the pupils spend all the day with similar pupils. Even within sets or streams the ability and needs of pupils will vary so you must take account of these. They may range from lack of speed in completing a task to a severe problem which requires one-to-one help. For those for whom an IEP exists, the targets in it need to be subsumed in the class planning.

Where pupils are considered gifted or talented, there are unlikely to be similar explicit plans, but you must consider the challenge such pupils need, or have sufficient supplementary work to keep them interested and busy. You must also consider the needs of any pupils whose English is not fluent; will they need help with instructions or recording, concept development or vocabulary? You may need to differentiate work for them or prepare special materials.

You must consider the pace of every individual pupil's learning, not every day or every lesson, but the planning must address this. You must ensure that the tasks have increasing difficulty and vary them. For instance, poster drawing is popular with both primary and secondary schools as a way of seeing whether pupils have grasped the point or recognise the issues around a topic. Unless such a task moves on, develops, it becomes a time-consuming exercise that challenges no one except those with little artistic talent. Think through sticking points when relating pupils to subject matter concerned. You can often pre-empt trouble spots and trouble makers with a little forward planning. Where or with whom might you need detailed instructions repeated on a board somewhere, where will you need increased explanations? Thinking it through beforehand can allow you to make time slots for the extra bits, or find different resources to support certain pupils and prevent them from being disruptive.

Planning an individual lesson

Even if you are not doing the planning of whole lessons with the teachers, many HLTAs are. They have prior discussion with the teacher about the medium- and short-term plan intentions, and their ideas are part of the teacher's overall planning for that group of pupils. Although you may not plan in the great detail I am about to describe, I shall go through the whole process, showing you that each part has a meaning. Once you grasp these principles you will internalise the process and it will be second nature. You may only plan some parts in detail, the actual format of the paper plan being immaterial – it needs to work for you. It can be landscape or portrait, A3 or A4, have boxes, work vertically or horizontally, it doesn't matter one bit (see Figure 7.2).

Elliott uses the technique of a timeline adapted from those of the DfES to describe the various patterns diagramatically that lessons can take (Elliott 2004b: 67). They are basically variations on the three-part lesson, with a starter, a middle, main, activity and a plenary or closing part. The main part can be in two sections with a short plenary or whole-class discussion in the middle, and groups can work on various tasks or the same one. The way in which this all came over in the national strategies made it seem a formal, essential structure all taking place within an hour. The Literacy Hour has become an established rigid routine in most schools, to the detriment of imagination, creativity and need. Flexibility went out of the window. The purpose of such a plan as was suggested was exactly as the title of the book covering it intended – a framework. It certainly helped teachers used to total flexibility where lessons never seemed to end, where pupils thought they had all day or even all week to complete a task, and enabled structured planning to take place. The point is that lessons need to start and finish and serve a purpose, so a starting activity and a finishing one need to be there as well as the main activity. The timing of the various parts will depend on the time allowed for the whole lesson on the timetable and the nature of the tasks or activities proposed (see Figure 7.2).

Ideally a lesson plan will contain various elements:

The intention of the lesson – the learning objective
The way you intend opening the lesson – the starter
    How you will find out what the pupils remember – establishing prior learning
The main activities – with estimated times
    Any skills training
    Any differentiation
    Any grouping
    Any SEN, EAL, G&T
    Clearing-up time
Finishing activity including homework
Role of any other adults
Monitoring and assessment strategies and records to be kept
Resources needed
    Including lists of key words
Risk assessment
Evaluation and reporting strategy.

The actual choice of activities which will take the main focus of the lesson is a major decision. Part of the decision will depend on the long-term and medium-term plans, to ensure variety of experience a over the year. This is particularly important in subjects like art or music where the pupils should experience a range over the year. SOWs are really helpful not only in suggesting a range but also in a distribution of the range between the appropriate subject matter and the year, and choices will also depend on the age and stage of the pupils. There is an interesting table in MacGilchrist *et al.* (1997: 43 from Armstrong 1994: 52) where the suggested activities, teaching materials and instructional strategies are categorised under the headings of intelligences. Different activities can address different styles of learning.

There may be some lessons where there is a clear continuation from the last one, such as a DT project lesson where the models were half finished. The pupils know from the previous lesson that they have to get out the unfinished work and the tools and materials needed and get cracking; there will be no gathered starting activity where the class assemble for the teacher to input. The pupils will need warning as to the progression of time in order to clear away and get instructions for next time, but the plan will have extended over several school periods.

Date............... Teacher.............................. HLTA.. Year group...............

Lesson.................... Time........................... Place................................. Ability group........................

Number............

<u>Learning objective</u>

<u>Activities</u>
Starter

Main activity   **Grouping**   **Individual needs**

Finisher

Homework
Resources

Risk assessment

Other adult(s)

Comments:

Figure 7.2 A prototype plan for an anonymous lesson – to be adapted for any purpose

Pre-lesson organisation
You need to consider the following:

What rules need to be obeyed?
What rewards and sanctions operate in the class you will be taking?
How will you encourage independent learning?
What metacognitive strategies will you use?
How will you minimise disruption and delay?
What noise levels will be appropriate?
What routines will you use for controlling discussion and allowing pupils to ask questions?
What room will you be in? How is the room you will use organised?
How is the heating and ventilation controlled?
Will you need to move the furniture? Before or during the session?
How are the resources organised?
Does the room have the appropriate ICT facilities for you: OHP, a video player and television or interactive whiteboard and laptop?
Can the pupils move about the room if necessary? Can you move round the classroom?
What are the clearing-up routines?
What are the time constraints imposed by the school systems?
Are the displays important to your lesson?
Are there particular safety issues to consider, as compulsory in a laboratory?
Will a clothes change be needed as for PE? Will the pupils need to get out equipment?

The teacher will set the scene of his or her classroom, creating resource centres, setting out the furniture appropriately and putting up displays to create the atmosphere he or she feels is most conducive to the tasks to be performed there. Remember, you will always be working under the direction of the teacher, who takes responsibility for the learning of the pupils and so also the learning environment. He or she may delegate things to you; that is, you may be given a particular role in maintaining the environment, for example, display or plants and animals. The teacher may have other people doing other things, say art media and books, or have specialist technicians for science equipment or ICT, so you need to know how you fit into their scheme of things. If you feel you want to change things when you take the class you must negotiate this properly. Most teachers feel a bit about their room how we all feel about our homes: a bit possessive.

Some examples of good practice in thinking things through

The teacher wanted to use the whiteboard with pupils facing her at the beginning of the lesson but wanted them in groups for the tasks. The Year 3 class completely altered the room layout in a couple of minutes because they were trained in previous sessions how to lift, a sequence for the moves and the end product. They put the tables and chairs back equally quickly at the end of the lesson.

A Year 2 class were used to working in groups around tables but had become very chatty whatever the task, individual or group work. The teacher reorganised the tables to a basic U shape with an inner straight line. In this way she could make eye contact with the pupils more easily and encourage the children to work independently.

An HLTA taking a class found the Year 6 class tended to stampede the box of resources placed on the back workbench. She moved it to a more central point and got the children to come a group at a time.

An HLTA in a Year 8 class kept the textbooks for use on his desk until they were needed. He described the task to be done, and wrote the page they would need for information on the board. While still talking about the task, reminding them of the main points, he walked round the classroom with the pile and gave the texts out in sets of six for key students to distribute.

An HLTA in a laboratory made sure the resources used for the lesson were back in their appropriate boxes and counted the boxes in before summing up at the end of the lesson. The scissors were returned to a block which had holes corresponding to the number of scissors available. A glance sufficed to see all were back.

An HLTA about to take a Year 10 class broke off from coffee break early to make sure the laptop was loaded with the correct software and switched on, and that the proper pens were in place for the interactive whiteboard.

Learning objective

The main purpose of the plan is to ensure that the pupils progress according to some predetermined intention as easily, interestingly and effectively as possible. The outcome may not be the intention but if your intention was clear, change from it will also be clear. Different schools have differing names for the learning intention of the lesson: learning aim or objective, desired learning outcome or some such. It matters not, the purpose is to be able to plan for what you want to happen and know whether you get there or not. It is going to help you enormously if you can see how this particular lesson fits into the large plan and you know what the final desired learning outcome is to be [2.3]. Are the pupils intended to sit an examination, learn skills to enable them to complete a task or even go for a particular job? Are they to learn to love the subject (music, say), learn to use the subject (as in a foreign language) or practise a skill (as in part of ICT)?

Elliott (2004b) suggests using Bloom's taxonomy when considering the tasks you choose for pupils. Bloom separated learning outcomes into three domains:

- Cognitive – knowing and understanding;
- Affective – feelings and attitudes;
- Psychomotor – the skills and behaviour side of learning.

It is very useful to recognise whether the outcome of the lesson you will take will be cognitive or behavioural, or may change feelings or attitudes. It immediately helps you to look for signs of success in the right place. Bloom also separated the cognitive domain into six areas which are hierarchical:

- Knowledge – of facts and words;
- Comprehension – understanding the concept underlying the words;
- Application – being able to use the material learnt in other contexts;
- Analysis – being able to take apart the ideas learnt to see what they are made of;
- Synthesis – being able to make up new ideas associated with what is learnt;
- Evaluation – being able to find and provide evidence to show the value of knowing or understanding something.

Too often tasks stop at the knowledge level, sometimes barely reaching the comprehension level. It is essential that the application level is reached otherwise the knowledge is just so much useless clutter. Hopefully, all six levels are reached from time to time as the series of lessons in a subject area accumulate. Elliott quotes a useful list from a DfES (2002c) publication of terms that you can use when actually defining learning objectives, based on the hierarchical taxonomy (see Table 7.1). Wording an objective appropriately indicates to the reader the level of challenge the activity might have.

There is a whole chapter on objectives in Cohen *et al.* (2004) where behavioural and non-behavioural objectives are analysed in some detail. They also remind readers of the mnemonic used for targets in relation to objectives: they should be SMART (specific, measurable, achievable, realistic and timebound).

Starting

There will be some lessons with a group you do not know. It will be your first time with them because of new timetabling, emergencies or the start of a new school year. Then you will have a longer starting session and put into your planning various things to establish before you start the lesson proper. This would include the rules to be obeyed when you are

Table 7.1 Defining learning objectives (Elliott 2004b: 62 from DfES 2002c)

Draw	State	Record	Recognize	Identify	Increasing
Sort	Describe	Select	Present	Locate information from text	difficulty
Decide	Discuss	Define	Classify	Explain what . . .	
Devise	Calculate	Interpret	Construct	Clarify	
Plan	Predict	Conclude	Solve	Determine the key points from . . .	
Formulate	Explain why	Use the pattern to . . .	Reorganize	Explain the difference between . . .	
Link/make connections between	Use the idea of . . . to . . .	Use a model of . . . to . . .	Provide evidence for . . .	Evaluate the evidence for . . .	

in charge, the rewards or sanctions system under which you will be operating, and your expectations of behaviour, noise levels and routines for asking questions and clearing up. It will depend on the age of the pupils whether you can just say all this at the beginning or whether, for instance, clearing-up routines will be established by slowly going through them at an earlier than usual clearing-up time. Establish with the pupils how they can clarify points about which they are unclear, when they can deviate from what you say, and how you want them to behave if there is an emergency. It may seem time-consuming, but time taken at this point in making routines you expect to be clear at the beginning establishes a way of working with that class that will last for the rest of your time with them. You will need to be consistent in your routines yourself, and always make sufficient time for these to be fulfilled.

Some teachers always start a lesson, or the whole day, with the register. This can be a dead time for the pupils and may provide the first opportunities for disruption. Many primary classes now have tasks written on the board, such as a small quiz or a reading task ready for the pupils as they come into the room. This allows them to settle while the teacher takes the register. This can be verbal or silent, on paper or using ICT. Many secondary schools now have computers networked with the office with class lists ready on them; all the teacher has to do is check this list at an appropriate time and send it to the office. Thus the process does not detract from the opening of the lesson. Most secondary schools seem to operate on a basis of pupils moving round the building between lessons and the teacher staying put because of the resourcing and equipment issues, particularly for PE, science and technology. This means you have to be prepared for a settling time, taking up as little lesson time as possible, and having strategies to deal with it.

The national strategies have many ideas for starter sessions, but it may be that you use this time to introduce a new subject, in a purely instructional session. However new the subject, there will still be an opportunity within it to recap what the pupils might already know in the area, to explore a linked subject. Even if the subject is not new, the pupils will not necessarily remember what they did or learnt last time, as things have happened to them since then. Whatever it is, the pupils will be at some point in their learning before you start and this will need to be determined, in addition to knowing where you want them to be at the end. The lesson will be a journey in time. You may want to make this recapping a more extended part of the lesson in order to find out how much the pupils already know, thus avoiding boring repetition. It will all depend on the subject, the timing in the overall plan of things and recommendations from the teacher. You can use oral questioning (which you should prepare beforehand), a quiz, even a test. If the work is to be practical, a skills practice session would be a good idea. You want to establish the knowledge base from which you are going to work and also how much the pupils understand, what their concept level is. Think through your questions and make them as open ended as possible, and consider how you deal with those whose answers are incorrect without discouraging them from trying again.

Whether this is to be a new subject, a repetition of an old one, or a continuation, it is essential that you point out to the pupils what the lesson hopes to achieve. Some teachers write the learning objective on the board at the beginning of the lesson; some also get the pupils to write it after the title on their written work. Thus anyone marking or reading the

Photograph 7.1   An HLTA registering pupils during a lull in the lesson

completed piece of work can understand why the recording and marking was done in a particular way.

The time given over to assessment of prior learning should be minimal as it involves repetition for some. Also, limit the time you spend on explaining and demonstrating, or on direct teaching, unless you intersperse it with some kind of interactive work. It is just like listening to lectures or talks; you may switch off after five minutes unless something catches your imagination.

Main activities

The activity itself should have a shape: introduction, the activity itself and review. Practical subjects will have elements of skills, knowledge and understanding, just as the more formal activities. You should be trained by the teacher in any skills with which you are unfamiliar. The task may be practical, with apparatus or resources of some kind, or talking or writing, or it can be games, drawing or completing a worksheet. It is tempting to give the less able the easier, more mundane, activities, but they are just as easily bored as the others. Make it clear from the outset what the timeframe for the activity is and what warning of clearing-up time you will give. Ensure pupils know what the expected outcome will be, for example a completed list, a started essay, a practised skill, a set of discussion points or just experience. How are they to record their findings if it is an experiment, what will happen to their work at the end of the session, what will the plenary involve: reporting back, questions raised or a summary of what has been done? Above all make sure they know why they are doing the task: is it to reinforce or repeat something already done, to solve a problem, to enrich their understanding, to learn more or to revise?

You will have planned differentiated tasks where you want them, and grouped pupils to help each other where that is important. Have subsidiary tasks up your sleeve for the early finishers and strategies ready for those who do not finish. Planning for a range of work rates could include differentiation of either task completion rates, or available resources and support. Make sure you do remind them of the passing of time appropriately and give enough time for clearing up, searching the floor for loose items, washing up, returning books or resources and dealing with any end products. It is not the role of teacher, TA or technician to clear up a room.

Differentiation is about matching the lesson to the ability of the pupils concerned. This needs to be carefully integrated into the planning. Try the checklist below (Table 7.2) with your teachers when planning. Differentiation is not just about making a different work-sheet for some pupils (see Examples 7.1, 7.2); remember, supporting pupils undertaking tasks is not teaching unless you extract the teaching points from them.

Assessments and record keeping

You do need to plan how you or the teacher will know whether the objective has been successful. The measures you use are called success criteria. If you have thought these through beforehand, it is so much easier to recognise success or the lack of it. You could add these to your plan or put it in the comments lines at the bottom, then all you have to do is to note the level of success.

You also have to plan for any assessment of individual pupils. This may not take place every lesson but only at the end of a group of lessons. Teachers may advocate end of topic tests, exercise books may have to be marked or models assessed, words learnt or pages read may need to be recorded; you will follow the school's systems. You may need to note success at reaching IEP targets or particular incidents; for the teacher, just note on your plan, then you will have a reminder in front of you in the module of all the activity.

Ensure that you know the role of any other adults in the room, and that they are aware of what will be going on, and make sure they have a role during the starting and finishing time. Remember, the 'Velcro'™ approach to learning support by TAs is not the best way to deal with pupils' needs; the Code of Practice clearly states 'that this may not be the most appropriate way of helping the child' (DfES 2001: 53). So when planning on knowing when a TA will be in the room, involve him or her just as you would wish to be involved in similar circumstances. It may only be a quick word at the beginning of the lesson, but you should know where you can point the TA to assist a group rather than an individual, or what the TA can do to allow his or her 'charges' to have a go on their own. Develop those

Table 7.2   Differentiation checklist from DfES (2002a: 63) (adapted from Dickson and Wright 1996)

Focus	Strategies	How I use these strategies
Resources	Selected for: – appropriate readability; 　　　　　 – levels; 　　　　　 – ease of use by pupils; 　　　　　 – good design. Wide variety of media. Use of technology. Use of study guides. Well-managed storage and retrieval systems. Pupil preparation. Study skills built into course programme.	
Tasks	Providing a variety of tasks. Matching of tasks to abilities, aptitudes and interests. Ensuring children stay on task. Identifying the outputs that tasks lead to. Providing a range of tasks to allow for choice. Building learning routes.	
Support	Support from other adults and children. Individual support from the teacher. Support from carefully resourced systems and technology. Celebration of achievement. Co-operative 'partnership' teaching. Small-group teaching.	
Response	Informing children of desired learning outcomes. Making assessment criteria explicit. Response partners (pupils working in pairs). Learning logs. Small-group tutoring. Individual action plans. Response reflects what the child has previously achieved.	

alternative ways of communication other than the last minute chat that you may have found useful; try to seek them out in breaktime, or have an extra copy of the lesson plan, exercise books with messages, and post-its.

Finishing

Just letting pupils go because the bell goes, shouting homework over the rustle of coats, is not good practice. Ensure you have worked out how long you need, not only for clearing up, but also to reinforce the learning points of the lesson, to get feedback from the pupils and to note any questions the activity may have produced. The pupils will need time to feed back results to their peers and share ideas, which all help to consolidate the learning. Homework may be appropriate to your circumstances.

Game parks

Game parks are areas where hunters cannot kill wild animals. The government of Kenya manages the Serengeti Park carefully so that visitors can see some of the most beautiful animals in the world roaming free. The Serengeti covers an area of roughly 38000 km².

The food web below shows some of the important animals in the Serengeti.

a Which animals do lions eat?

b Which animals eat grass?

c A drought would reduce the amount of grass in the park. What effect would this have on the animals in the park? Explain your answer carefully.

d A disease has reduced the number of wildebeest. How would this affect
   – the lions? Why?
   – the zebras? Why?

Serengeti Game Park food web

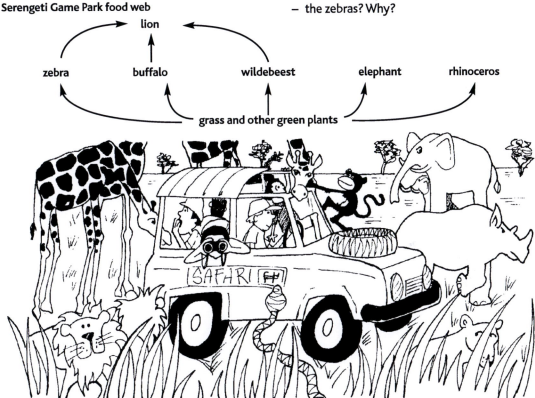

Animal	Number in 1000 km²
lion	20
wildebeest	6400
zebra	4800
buffalo	600
elephant	32
rhinoceros	2

Animal	Average adult mass (kg)
lion	300
wildebeest	230
zebra	230
buffalo	550
elephant	3200

Use the data in the tables to answer the following questions.

e Which is the commonest animal in the Serengeti?

f Which is the rarest animal in the Serengeti?

g There are about 750 lions in the Serengeti Park. Work out the total mass of all the lions.

h About how many zebras are there in the Serengeti?

i Work out the total mass of all the zebras.

j Explain why the total mass of zebras is much bigger than the total mass of lions.

Example 7.1 A worksheet for more able pupils

Game Parks

Game parks are areas where hunters cannot kill wild animals. The government of Kenya manages the Serengeti Park carefully so that visitors can see some of the most beautiful animals in the world roaming free. The food web below shows some of the important animals in the Serengeti.

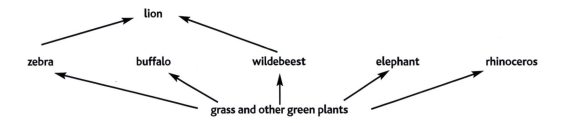

Using the food web answer the following questions

(a) Which animals do lions eat?_____

(b) Which animals eat grass?_____

(c) What effect on the animals would a drought cause?

_____

_____

_____

(d) A disease has reduced the number of wildebeest. How would this
     affect

1 the lions?

_____

_____

_____

2 the zebras?

_____

_____

_____

Example 7.2   The same worksheet differentiated for lower ability pupils

Photograph 7.2 An HLTA taking a class with another TA supporting pupils

Resource preparation

One of the joys of having HLTAs, the schools tell me, is to have assistants who can prepare resources that the teachers do not have time to do. Hopefully, the time you put into this is recognised, that you have non-pupil contact time to do this aspect of the work, and when you do, it is invaluable. I have seen differentiated worksheets prepared by TAs, and displays, models, posters and games. Some have prepared vocabulary lists for the wall and individual ones for pupils who need them, others have sorted out the textbooks needed or visited the library for extra resources, and some have brought in artefacts from home or found relevant websites.

When preparing equipment and tools you need to know the degree of accuracy for measuring purposes, whether for preparing materials, measuring with the pupils or for pupils' recording. You must familiarise yourself with any tools or apparatus to be used before you use them with the pupils.

Make sure you have resources ready before you work with the pupils, unless getting out the equipment is part of the task, which may be so in science or PE. The resources should be of the highest quality that is available. You and the equipment are examples for the students so do not use tatty books, mend them or ask if they can be disposed of. Your care,

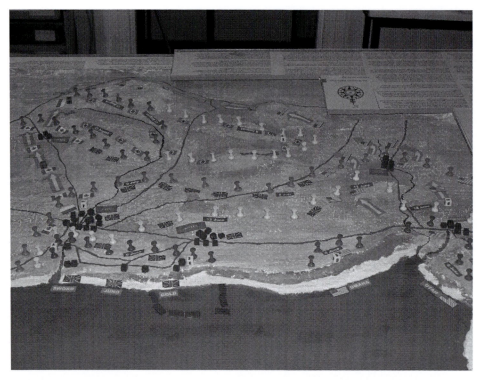

Photograph 7.3   A model of the D-Day landings in the Second World War prepared by
an HLTA

and the safe and appropriate use of tools, sets an example. Discuss with the teacher or line
manager any problems with materials; the allocation, location, quality and availability of
equipment; or even the space you have to work in – if you do not say, people will presume
all is well. Also, tell the teacher if pupils break anything, as the school may well have a
policy that pupils pay for replacements if breakage was deliberate. Dealing with broken
glass or spilt liquids needs to be done safely and you may need to summon help.

Risk assessment

Make sure you are aware of the safety measures you and the pupils need to take with any
activity [3.3.8]. Usually, pupils enjoy any kind of practical work, whether it means using
tools or media, or working with their own bodies as in PE or drama. You will certainly be
using electrical equipment at some time and it is especially important that you follow the
safety precautions and instructions for such equipment, as you will probably be using it
with pupils at some time or leaving it for colleagues to use. All items will have come into
school with a handbook for their safe and proper use. Follow the setting-up and operating
instructions indicated for the machine you are using, as some actions can damage equipment. Be careful yourself and discourage pupils from standing in the beam of projectors
and looking directly at the source. In order to minimise risks, also be alert for things like
the use of the correct furniture.

   If you are planning to take pupils out of school do make sure you know all about the risk
assessments that have to be done. Risk assessment concerning use of chemicals, tools,

apparatus, living materials, and so on is a must for all science and practical lessons and all lessons taken outside the confines of the normal classroom. Consult with your teachers about this, as there are probably some very simple forms and completed assessments for routine events. The Association for Science Education (ASE) literature is very useful in this area and their safety documents are essential for all schools (ASE 1996; 2001).

Reflection and feedback

It is important as in all of your work to reflect on the day's work and feed back to the teacher in charge of the group or groups you have been working with. The ways in which you do this feedback will have been negotiated when you were asked to do the lesson: it may be a verbal 'all was well' or it may be a note at the end of your plan. Keep copies of your plan with the notes you make on them in a ringfile because they are often useful on a second occasion. It is interesting to realise that although the same topic will recur, it is very rare for the same lesson to happen, as a different group of pupils a year later will receive the same instructions and use the same apparatus with quite different outcomes. This is what makes teaching so interesting and fulfilling. The supply teacher self-study guide (DfES 2002a) has a useful checklist for planning on page 60. It suggests you check:

- Coverage – is there sufficient breadth and balance?
- Progression – in the learning objectives for the subject involved?
- Age relevance – for the intended pupils?
- Clarity – could other people understand them?
- Suitability – are they in line with the school aims and the learning environment within the classroom?

Essential reading

Any subject curriculum handbook for teachers which accompanies any published scheme being used in the school by your class or teachers you work.

ASE (1996) *Safeguards in the School Laboratory* (10th edn). Hatfield: Association for Science Education.

ASE (2001) *Be Safe: Health and Safety in Primary School Science and Technology*. Hatfield: Association for Science Education.

Any school guidance on health and safety and taking pupils out of class.

Some further reading

DfES (2001) *Special Educational Needs Code of Practice*. London: Department for Education and Skills.

Elliott, P. (2004a) 'Communication in the classroom', in V. Brooks, I. Abbott and L. Bills (eds) *Preparing to Teach in Secondary Schools*. Maidenhead and New York: Open University Press and McGraw-Hill Education, pp. 59–72.

Elliott, P. (2004b) 'Planning for learning', in V. Brooks, I. Abbott and L. Bills (eds) *Preparing to Teach in Secondary Schools*. Maidenhead and New York: Open University Press and McGraw-Hill Education.

Hayes, D. (2000) *The Handbook for Newly Qualified Teachers: Meeting the Standards in Primary and Middle Schools*. London: David Fulton Publishers (chapter on 'Lesson planning and preparation', pp. 58–72).

Hayes, D. (2003) *Planning, Teaching and Class Management in Primary Schools* (2nd edn). London: David Fulton Publishers (the early part, pp. 1–27).

Kyriacou, C. (1998) *Essential Teaching Skills* (2nd edn). Cheltenham: Stanley Thornes Ltd (chapter on planning, pp. 16–30).

Pollard, A. (2002) *Reflective Teaching: Effective and Evidence-informed Professional Practice*. London and New York: Continuum (chapter on planning, pp. 192–215).

Useful websites

www.curriculumonline.gov.uk for curriculum support materials

www.dfes.gov.uk for the latest educational news and links to other sites

www.dfes.gov.uk/leagateway to find your LEA website

www.nc.uk.net for curriculum information and support materials for inclusion, SEN and G&T

www.ngfl.gov.uk for general gateway to educational resource

www.qca.org.uk for support materials, especially schemes of work and assessment information

www.standards.dfes.gov.uk for statistics and strategy materials

www.teachernet.gov.uk for support materials and documents in general

Subject association websites

Design and technology: www.data.org.uk – Design and Technology Association

English: www.nate.org.uk – National Association of Teachers of English

Mathematics: www.m-a.org.uk and www.atm.org.uk – Mathematics Association and the Association of Teachers of Mathematics

Science: www.ase.org.uk – Association for Science Education

Also useful is the ICT support website: www.becta.org.uk – British Educational Communications and Technology Agency, a UK agency supporting ICT developments.

CHAPTER 8

Performance

When it actually comes to standing in the classroom and 'delivering a lesson' it is like going on a stage. You will have read and partially learnt the script, you have an audience whose reception could be anything from eager to hostile, you will have props and lots of support from other members of the stage crew, and you should be well prepared and probably well rehearsed. You will probably have worked in the location for some time, you will know quite a bit about the audience, and you are in charge! You have authority, so have confidence.

There are several things to bear in mind. Relationships with the pupils and communication are at the crux of what you have to do, and you have dealt with individual pupils and groups for some time. As these are well covered in the increasing number of books now available for TAs I shall not go into detail about them here but concentrate on managing whole-class sessions. The first HLTA book went into some detail about the kinds of relationships you have with pupils in whatever kind of grouping you are working, and previous chapters have focused on the purposes of lessons and all the planning and preparation you can do to provide the best background to the lesson. This chapter will look at the personal characteristics you need to develop when undertaking direct teaching, the performance or acting skills you need to achieve the best results. You are not there just to 'babysit' or cope but to make a difference to as many of the pupils in the class as you can.

The confidence bit is half the battle. Elliott points out the importance of how we communicate non-verbally how we feel about ourselves, the pupils and the subject, and how well organised, and competent confident we are [3.3.2]. He gives some simple guidelines to help:

- Stand or sit confidently – shoulders back, spine straight and so on;
- Stand still! Shifting feet distracts pupils and are a sure sign of nerves;
- Control your hands! However nervous you are feeling inside, try to avoid fidgeting with them;
- Try to be positive and expressive with your face: smile and nod regularly when pupils say and do anything positive;
- Have the confidence to approach pupils for an intimate discussion of their work, but avoid invading their personal space;

Photograph 8.1   An HLTA getting down to a pupil's height to make eye contact

- With smaller pupils in particular, it is much better to squat next to them rather than lean over them when having a one-to-one interaction.

  The way that you use your body will not only influence the way that you are perceived, but also the way that you feel. If you can act confident, even when feeling nervous, you are likely to end up feeling more confident.

  (Elliott 2004a: 99)

It is not just a question of presence. Elliott also points out that the way you dress, organise your paperwork, your punctuality, also add to the way in which you are perceived by pupils. Dress and organisation give out messages; remember, you are a very powerful role model. If you want tidiness and organisation from the pupils in their attitude to the classroom, their written work and their practical application, you have to model this.

He continues in his chapter to point out that habits that teachers can develop during 'delivery' of a lesson can be either helpful or not. He talks of territory: just as the pupils have personal space, so do you. Use the whole room, but avoid talking while moving around: the movement indicates that the whole room is your territory, but talking while moving is very distracting. Talking from different parts of the room keeps the pupils on their toes, but stop to do it and make sure you have their attention; they should have their faces towards you, even if you speak from the back of the class. Standing by resources when you are referring to them is very helpful, as it locates the place for the pupils, but watch out that you do not stand in front of the very poster, screen or board that you are referring to.

Talking and listening

When people think of teaching they envisage a person standing at the front of a group of people and instructing them. This is part of the act, but hopefully you will have realised that when on the receiving end of a lecture, a purely instructional talk, your concentration may slip after about five minutes. This is why lecturers use so many slides, and why good teachers ensure there is some interaction with the listeners. This interaction may be through the use of visual aids like slides, films or artefacts or, usually in schools, tasks where the pupils have to actually do something or talk themselves to ensure they are actively involved in the lesson. Taking notes in lectures is one way that older students keep focused, as well as having a written aide memoire to carry away with them. Having a question and answer session of some kind is the most common way of interacting with one's audience, gaining their attention and hopefully their interest. It is also a way of gaining information about where the pupils' thinking is currently.

Distinct kinds of classroom talk
Where you have a good relationship with a teacher and he or she can take time to observe and discuss your observations, see if you can record the types of talking and how much of the lesson is used proportionately in each of the following:

Cognitive talk – about a subject
Managerial talk – organising the session
           – dealing with behaviour
Counselling talk – responding to pupils' needs or feelings
Expressive talk – voicing your feelings about a subject or situation.

It is very important that you make time to listen as well as talk. Unless pupils are able to articulate their thoughts they will not have fully understood what the subject is about. This does not mean they have to talk all the time, or every time; work this out for yourself. If every pupil in a class of 30 is an individual and has individual needs, and your role is to instruct, how many pupils can tell you what they feel or understand in an hour's lesson? Not many! And those who do articulate will be the most vocal ones. You have to work out how over several lessons you can gain all views and enable each pupil to feel valued and heard. Written work is one way, provided the pupils can write and the written work is such that they can air their views and not just give results or complete a particular task. The best thing is to gain the pupils' confidence in you as a listener and as someone who is fair. Make sure the quiet ones are able to answer questions. Pollard (2002) states that on average a class teacher waits only two seconds before either repeating a question, rephrasing it, redirecting it or extending it. Pace is important but so is allowing pupils time to think; can you answer everything in two seconds? Be very careful of how you respond if answers are wrong; take time in a lesson to talk quietly directly to pupils who might get overlooked. Keep notes separately on how each is responding and giving opinions, or replying or asking questions over a period of time.

Differentiation is not just a skill of adjusting worksheets but applies to how you talk to each member of the class, wording your language for differing abilities, understanding and background. Inclusion is not just having difficult or different pupils present in the room. The ways in which you talk to one or two groups or to the whole class can help the slow learners in one instance and challenge the bright sparks in another, and you can speak clearly and slowly for any pupil with EAL.

Always be on the lookout for a learning opportunity for the class as a whole or individuals, and be prepared to jot things down on the planning sheet as you go along, a quick reminder. Actively listen so that the pupils know you will hear what they say and take account of it. Give the pupils time to articulate what they want to say, they will not be as able to express themselves as you are. Tone of voice is often as important as actual words and can indicate whether you will bother about or dismiss what has been said. Positive phrasing of responses may need a bit of thought:

> 'Thanks for that, that might be one way of looking at it, anyone else got any ideas?'
> 'Well tried'
> 'Any other ideas?' 'Try again'

These are all better than saying 'No!'

Never laugh at a pupil unless that is the intention and mood of the lesson, for instance a drama lesson, it can be totally demoralising. Humour in teaching is essential, but like behaviour management strategies it should not be directed at people. Wrong answers or daft questions may give you quite an insight into the pupils' thinking or mood.

The other prerequisite about talking to a whole class is the use of your voice. There are various techniques that are useful in instructing delivery, but it is important to remember that your voice exists because you have vocal chords in your throat. These chords are muscles just like your leg muscles; they can get overused and strained just like leg muscles, and can be cared for. Some teacher training establishments actually give their students a session with a speech therapist for tips to help them maintain vocal health. It is well known that singers, politicians and teachers are prone to trouble with their voice. Sore throats, hoarseness, loss of voice and even the development of non-malignant nodules can occur more frequently for these groups of people because their voices are used such a lot and can be misused. Singers warm up and practise regularly, and if they are ill it takes time to get their voices back to full working order. Your voice will be less used on holiday, and then suddenly you are using it all day, every day, back at work. Playground duty can wreak havoc if you have to shout the length of the playground to stop a child climbing somewhere he or she shouldn't. Taking sips of water to lubricate your throat can help, and recognising your voice level is important. If you are having any troubles, seek advice from a speech therapist. He or she may recommend avoiding certain dietary items, such as dairy products, which can produce a lot of mucus in your throat, or recommend particular exercises that might help.

The way you use your voice with a class is important. You may have realised when watching teachers at work that if they speak quietly, they are more likely to have a quiet class. The shouters tend to have a noisy class and then need to shout more to get themselves heard.

Pitch is important, and speed and the way in which you express yourself and project your voice all have an impact, good or bad. You may have to raise your voice to get heard in the first place, but a loud voice all the time will enable the pupils to chat and still pay attention when they need to. Do ensure you speak clearly, slowly enough to enunciate properly, but quickly enough to keep attention. Change your voice levels for effect; if you can act different voices use them sparingly but for effect. You may have also noticed that female newsreaders tend to have lower pitched voices. These seem to be both clearer and more pleasant to listen to, so you might like to ask a friend to comment on yours or tape record it and listen to it yourself.

As with dress and organisation, you really do need to try to be a role model in your language. Regional accents are pleasant and must be retained, but some dialects do have some incorrect grammatical phrasing. This is a very sensitive issue, as we are trying to get the pupils to write correct grammatical language, and we would consider 'them things' to be incorrect. Correcting spoken language should be done carefully, and probably individually, very quietly. Young children often get tenses and participles of verbs wrong, saying things like 'I runned home'. Parents usually just repeat what the child has said but say it correctly, 'I ran home', and don't make a big issue over it, and they also use the correct form of speech themselves. Soon the child says it the correct way without even realising he or she has been corrected. This could be a problem for you if you retain some of your local idioms which are ungrammatical. If you are brave, talk to a friend or mentor about this; role modelling is a powerful tool for a teacher.

A brief word of warning: Elliott (2004) points out that the teacher in front of the class is in a position of power. While it may seem that this is a totally good thing, as you need power to control youngsters, particularly when authority seems to be more and more disregarded and preventing disruption the main concern, it can be abused. Use the power or your position responsibly, build good relationships and encourage trust.

Starting

The last chapter talked about planning a starter, but how you actually enter the room or allow the pupils to enter the room can set the tone for the rest of the lesson. This may sound a bit secondary to some of you who work in primary but the same is true of all entries to the classroom, in the morning, after break or lunch. If you are having clear lesson boundaries in primary classes, make sure the pupils understand the break, and allow them to stand up and stretch their legs, wave their arms, have a chat, visit the loo, what a course would call a comfort break; you need it and so do they. Remember the sections about blood circulating and getting oxygen to the brain; why not take them out and run round the playground three times and come back in again then have a new start to the new subject? Both you and the pupils will sense the tone immediately by body language. You will tell whether the break has been incident free and they can tell whether you are prepared and confident.

> Be punctual and ready.
> Ensure the pupils enter in an orderly fashion, not necessarily single file, but not pushing, shoving and shouting.
> Have a routine for where pupils sit, and put their coats and bags and personal belongings like pencil cases.
> Have a routine about touching things you may have put out on the desk, to get on with them or not to touch.
> Have appropriate things on the board ready: the date, the lesson objective, the pages they need, instructions, a mini-test, whatever.
> Do you greet them? Do they stand when you come in the room if they come in first?

If the class is new to you, establish your own rules as soon as possible, although you may be restricted by the rules established by the class teacher. If there is a real clash of opinion, say on levels of noise that you find intolerable for the work in hand, discuss it with the class teacher at the earliest opportunity. Learn all the children's names as soon as you can, not just the names of children who impose themselves on you. Hayes has a useful checklist of classroom conventions for new teachers to think about; try talking the following through with the teacher before you take over the class for the first time if possible, then you will not have problems:

- conversation
- possessions
- movement around the room
- movement outside the room
- taking turns
- choosing
- team games
- volume of talk
- manners
- relating to adults
- care of equipment
- choosing partners
- the production of drafts and practice pieces
- the quality of final products
- dealing with finished work
- sharpening pencils
- going to the toilet.

(Hayes 2003: 23)

Photograph 8.2   A TA using a signal convention to stop a task in order to make a point

Hayes also gives some things to avoid:

- Being bombarded with questions
- Courting short-term popularity
- Attempting too much too soon
- Trying to make a big impression.

(Hayes 2000: 43)

As you are taking over teacher's class, it is likely that many of the parameters for success will already have been set out in the planning: the pace, the amount you are expecting to get through in the lesson, the kind of resources available, the ways in which you can ensure success. But, fairly quickly, you will put your personal imprint on the lessons you take, and the pupils will know whether you are a 'soft touch' or you mean what you say.

An example of good practice

The policy of the primary school was to 'grow their own' TAs. While appointments were open and fair, those who had acted as volunteers in the school had already been observed in the way they approached the work with the children and carried out the wishes of the teachers. As the TAs grew into the job, many opportunities for professional development were offered and performance management strategies employed for all staff, including the TAs. So when opportunities for more senior TAs came along, strengths could be recognised. Also, when teacher tasks were analysed the less curriculum focused, more administrative, tasks could be given to responsible, able TAs. Such times identified were the beginning of the day and the afternoon session when registers were taken, minor problems sorted out, lunch procedures determined and news shared. Where it was clear that the TAs could manage this well on their own, the teachers were able to take these periods of time away from the classroom. Gradually, one TA with particular curriculum expertise was asked to undertake some formal teaching during this time during short starter sessions, so that when the teacher returned, the class were ready for instructional input. These sessions were carefully jointly planned, and the resulting increase in time available for the teacher became her PPA time. The children looked forward to the sessions, the changeover was seamless because of the planning, and the resulting level of understanding from the children increased. The TA was able to stay on in the class for the rest of the morning and slide back into a supportive role. She was only able to take the starter role because of her capability in settling the children, her curriculum knowledge, her relationship with the class teacher and the joint planning.

The way in which the actual lesson begins will have been planned with the teacher. You may be going to have a particular starter activity as recommended in national strategies, and this may or may not have anything directly to do with the main subject of the lesson. Hopefully, it is directly relevant so that the lesson has a coherence for the pupils; however, it could be a mental starter using tables, just to get the pupils' minds working while the lesson itself is going to deal with data handling or shape. You will have to discuss this with the teacher when planning. Give the starter its own shape if it is a separate sub-subject, with a beginning, middle and end, so that pupils know what they are doing, and why, and when it starts and finishes. Always indicate to the pupils the objective of any activity.

Questioning and challenging

The more conventional lessons described in the last chapter will open with some kind of recap or assessment activity so that the teacher can judge at what level the pupils are, what they have remembered from the previous lesson or year or school or what they can recall from life experiences. While there are some more formal ways of doing this, like tests or concept mapping (see the next chapter), a frequently used method is a verbal question and answer session. Questioning is a really important skill and may occur at any point in the lesson, not just at the beginning, and it may involve the whole class or just one pupil. Questioning needs practice, like any other skill, and the actual asking of the questions needs just the same kind of clarity, eye contact and structure as an exposition, although the timing is more crucial. When do you put in the question, how long do you wait for an answer, what do you do if no one answers or if they all do at once? You may need a strategy like 'hands up' even with a small group, or you could ask a pupil by name. Do not allow shouting out.

Questions can be categorised into open and closed, closed only having one possible answer. Often the aim is to make questions as open ended as possible, which means there can be several answers, immediately posing a challenge to those listening. Getting pupils to understand that the world is largely shades of grey, not black and white, is very helpful.

This means more pupils will offer answers, because they know they will not be proved wrong and lose face [3.3.3]. There are, of course, times when closed answers are needed, particularly in organisational questions or in, say, mathematics. Even here a rewording of a question, for example 'What is 2+2?' to 'How many ways can you make 4?', might make it both more interesting and more challenging. Hayes (ibid.) suggests other types of questions: asking for elaboration, offering leading questions or giving various alternatives within the question. He also suggests considering the purpose of a question, deciding what it is trying to achieve. Questions can focus attention, force comparisons, seek clarification, invite enquiry and seek explanations; they can also promote further learning by getting pupils thinking – you can probe their ideas, don't just accept the first thing they say. Pollard shows how questions can extend or lift ideas or funnel reasoning; how questioning can be sequenced to step up the intellectual challenge or move from problem solving to direct recall, or just be random (Pollard 2002: 286–89).

Can you challenge the answer to an open-ended question? For example:

'Why did the chicken cross the road?'
   'To get to the other side.'
'Why did it need to get to the other side?'
'What happened next?'
'Could somebody have carried it?'
'Was it on its own?' And so on.

You must also consider whether you will correct a pupil who gives a wrong answer to a closed question or will you ask others and seek a consensus? What sort of praise will you give if it is right? What will you do if they answer with another question? Listen to politicians, they are adept at this!

Watch a teacher in action and with their agreement,

Note the teacher's questions:
    Can you categorise them into open and closed?
    Who answers which ones?
    Do the same pupils always answer?

Note the pupils' questions:
    What kinds of questions do they ask?
    Are they organisational?
    Do they want more information?
    Do they indicate a depth of thought (the 'why' questions)?
    Do they try to divert the teacher from his or her purpose (part of attention seeking or deliberately distracting)?

Talk these findings over with the teacher after the lesson.
Do teachers use different kinds of questioning for different subjects?
Do different circumstances need different questions (emergencies, informal occasions or lessons)?

Photograph 8.3   A TA giving thinking time

You can plan questions just like any other part of the lesson. When actually asking them DO give the pupils thinking time, and time to articulate their thoughts. Sometimes you can take a vote on the answer, which might give you an idea as to how widespread a misconception is or how many of the class really know the answer. One technique teachers often seem to use is a question and answer session at the beginning of a lesson, not just to ascertain what the pupils know (or don't) but as a more interactive way of actually starting their exposition. Instead of just saying, 'You remember last week I said about Christopher Columbus . . .', they use the questions and answers to aid recall.

Some teachers have deliberately developed strategies for collecting pupils' questions. They know they cannot prolong a Q and A session because of various time constraints. Some have a questions board on which the pupils can put their questions in note form, or always have a pad of post-its ready, or they make themselves available after a class session in breaktimes. Following up such questions can be a really powerful way of making positive relationships with pupils using curriculum matters. Thompson and Feasey, when talking about science lessons, suggest teachers should encourage students to:

- generate a range of scientific questions;
- ask pertinent questions;
- appreciate that different kinds of questions can be answered in different ways;
- appreciate that not every question has one correct answer;
- develop a range of strategies to deal with different questions;

Photograph 8.4   The same TA later giving an explanation to the pupil

- question each other and themselves in a critical manner;
- support answers to questions using data from investigations or other sources;
- question the validity of their own and other data.

(quoted in Cohen *et al.* 2004: 238).

You can quickly see how this can be interpreted for other subjects.

Instructing and explaining

The key again is planning and preparation. These enable you to have confidence and to be clear. One of the odd things about learning is that until you have explained it to someone else you do not always have the right words in the right order to be clear, and often it is when that someone else challenges you or questions you that parts become clearer, or you realise that you have missed something out. It is by telling the pupils something that you will realise what it is exactly that you know and understand about the subject, but if you are not prepared you might not find this out until during the lesson, then you will be muddling the pupils as well as yourself! [3.3.2].

Accurate vocabulary is important, and not just to teach a foreign language. Science, in particular, has its own vocabulary and accuracy is even more important here than in a less investigative subject. If pupils are describing a poem or story, a Shakespearean play or an outing they have made they still need the right sort of words. Some time spent to plan thinking through vocabulary and any words they might need will not only help them to express their ideas but also help you to expound on the subject. Prepared word lists for any subject will help in spelling as well.

An example of good practice

A science TA in a secondary school has already prepared mini-lists for different subjects which she can hand out in a class lesson to those who need them. She has also prepared poster versions of the same lists for high permanent display in the laboratories where she works. Also in the photograph below are copies of the worksheets she had prepared after she had seen the teacher's planning.

Practise writing on a board and going to the back of the class to see if you can read it. Practise using an interactive whiteboard, loading it and saving any work that you do in the lesson. With the widespread use of these boards, as the software becomes available the need for video recorders and televisions will diminish, and will only be needed for those films or programmes that are not available on DVD. Use artefacts and pass them round, but

Photograph 8.5   The photograph shows posters and worksheets prepared by the TA

make sure they are returned. Drama is a very powerful learning tool useful even in subjects like science and mathematics to demonstrate concepts. Acting out the solar system in the playground, showing how electricity flows in a circuit or using costumes from the era you are describing can all help understanding.

There is a well-known maxim in teaching and lecturing: tell them what you are going to tell them, tell them, then tell them what you have told them. Basically, it means that you need to introduce a subject sometimes, giving the highlighted point of what you are going to cover, or scene setting, then you do the delivery, then you recap and remind the class what you have just been talking about. I have sat in HLTA lessons where the HLTA assumes that because the teacher has said something it is self-evident that the pupils will know it. This is not the case; teachers don't have a magic wand, much as they would like one. This summary at the beginning and end is not about the learning objective. While that should come as part of the introduction, the summary is about the process that you the speaker, or they the students, will go through in the next period of time, whatever constitutes the lesson.

In schools a pure lecture for a whole lesson is unlikely, owing to the concentration span of school-aged pupils. There will be time at some point for an informing section, describing and explaining. Kyriacou gives some key aspects which underpin effective explaining:

- *Clarity.* It is clear and pitched at the appropriate level.
- *Structure.* The major ideas are broken down into meaningful segments and linked together in a logical order.
- *Length.* It is fairly brief and may be interspersed with questions and other activities.
- *Attention.* The delivery makes good use of voice and body language to sustain attention and interest.
- *Language.* It avoids use of over-complex language and explains new terms.
- *Exemplars.* It uses examples, particularly ones relating to pupils' experiences and interests.
- *Understanding.* The teacher monitors and checks pupils' understanding.

(Kyriacou 1997: 42, 43)

Chairing a discussion

This can happen at a meal table with young children or as a formal debate with older primary and secondary pupils. It is a time when your role as a teacher takes second place, where the conversation is not teacher dominated. You are trying to elicit ideas and opinions from the pupils and enable them to argue with each other or share views amicably, you are being a chairperson. You may have to start such sessions off with questions, and some pupils may be uneasy or unaccustomed to having to share their views or defend them. You have to resist the temptation to give factual information that would disrupt the flow, and you may have to prepare the pupils for these kinds of sessions, get them to find out things or think about a topic before the lesson as homework, or research the area. Then you can start the ball rolling with a few open questions.

> ### Examples of good discussion practice
>
> A secondary class learning about slavery was asked to find out the good things about it for homework in order to be able to defend it in a debate. This meant not just accepting the current liberal view that all slavery is wrong. Why did it succeed for so long? Why do some countries or people still practise it? Why did the Americans have a civil war over the issue? The class discussion following the homework was much more informed and informative for the pupils than a direct lesson would have been.
>
> A primary school head decided that the conventional assembly taken once a week with the older children could be more profitably used as thinking time if the children led the debate. The previous experience of the children had been that all assemblies were listening time, so all you had to do was turn up, sit quietly, have a good sing for a bit, listen, maybe a short think if they were interested, and then they could go out to play; a largely inactive and relaxing time. It took the best part of a year and a half to break this habit, where the head introduced various topics, asked questions and allowed the children to voice opinions without offering ones in return. Increasingly, the head did not even need to bring up a topic. The children would come to the Friday sessions with their own questions, wanting their friends' and peers' views in order to clarify their own thinking. The head's role became one of selecting the 'hands up' to allow a speaker a chance to talk. The children were actively involved in discussing moral issues that had appeared during the previous week, either in their home or locally, gleaned from their parents' newspapers or television news. The head had to start and end the session appropriately for an assembly, but the discussions sometimes continued in the playground.

Skills teaching

The main thing to remember here is that you are trying to get the pupils to do the task for themselves, so demonstrate rather than carry out the task for them. Circulate carefully once you have set a class to a task, and if you find pupils struggling after you have demonstrated the process, be sensitive to the reason for the problem. If the work is careless, particularly if you know them well and they can do better, get them to do it again; if there is not time, at least recognise that they can do better. Maybe they are having an 'off' day. Check that they have the correct tools, and that the tools are fit for purpose. This even applies to pencils: an untidy piece of work may just be due to a blunt pencil! They may have misunderstood the whole-class demonstration, not paid sufficient attention or even not been able to see properly all the stages you showed. You are probably used to working with slower learning pupils, so be adept at supporting strategies which help but do not take over; sometimes a little help in the right place can move the pupil on to the next stage. A small child sewing on binca, the large mesh tapestry fabric, may cope very well until it comes to finishing off or threading a new needle.

Intervention and non-intervention

This is similar to the problem outlined above. You have to judge when it is helpful or important to interrupt a pupil whether they are struggling or in full flow [3.2.2]; it is about increasing the challenge of the exercise the pupil is doing. Usually judicious questioning is the appropriate way to interrupt: 'Have you thought any more about . . .?', 'Can you tell me what will happen next?', 'Could you improve on that bit there?' With the right pupils you can point out spellings as you monitor, as usually you will know the pupils well and know whether such a prompt is appropriate, and whether spelling is important in the task writing. Challenge is interesting; the deeper your challenge or intervention, the more emotional the resistance. Yet if learning is to have depth, affect the pupils' attitudes and engage their thinking, the challenge must sometimes be at this level (see Figure 8.1).

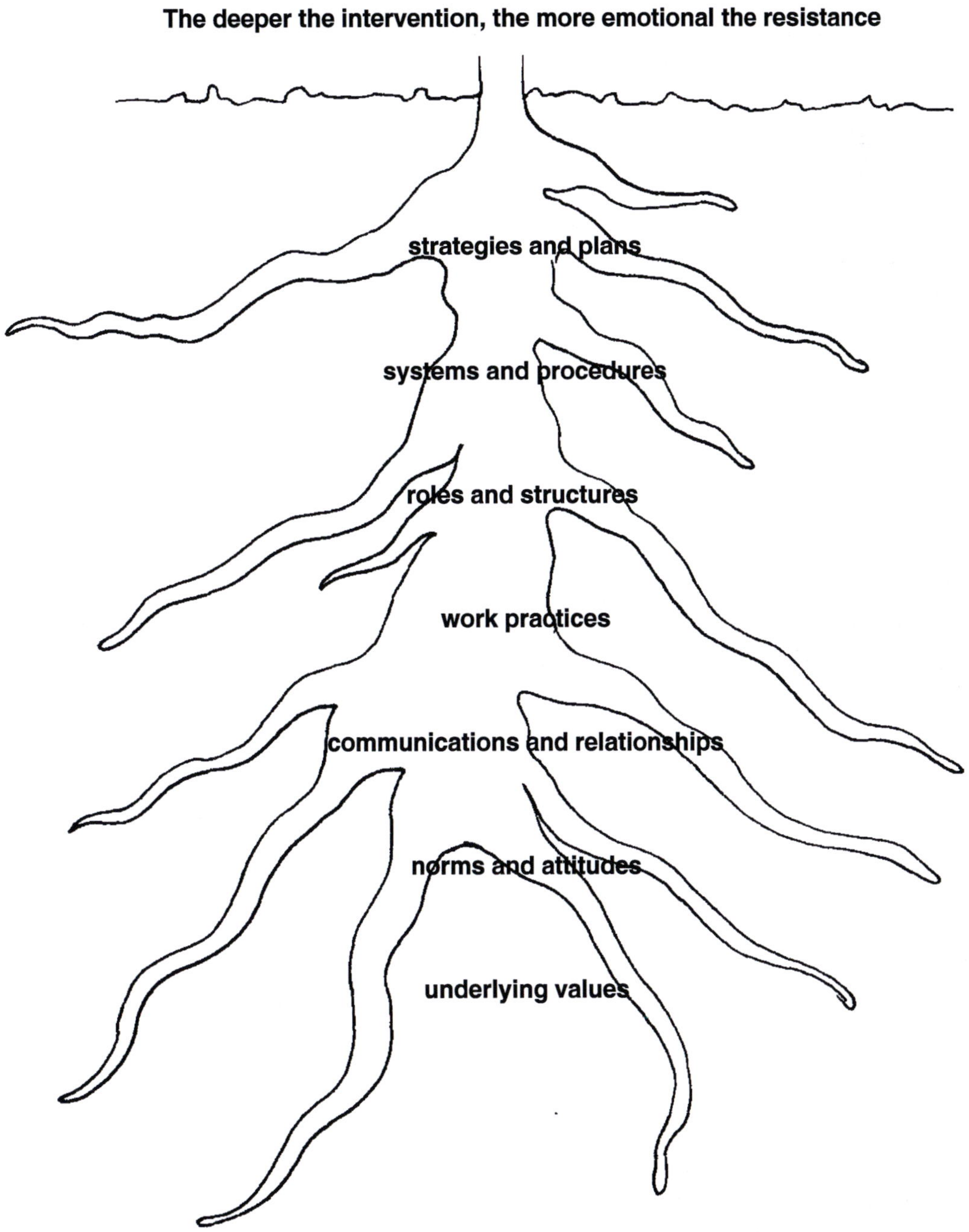

The deeper the intervention, the more emotional the resistance

strategies and plans

systems and procedures

roles and structures

work practices

communications and relationships

norms and attitudes

underlying values

Figure 8.1   Depths of intervention (from a lecture by Luke Abbott to Essex Advisers 1998)

Monitoring and feedback to pupils and teachers during a lesson

Whether or not you have to intervene you should be able to keep a weather eye on activity or passivity across the class [3.2.2]. Maintain eye contact with as many as possible if you are addressing them, as talking to the ceiling or reading notes does not engage your audience. You may have to resort to notes, most of us do, but have them arranged so that you only refer to them, and not read them. The only people who need to read notes are people who have had to publish their speeches beforehand because what they say will be an important legal record. Try putting the headings in bold, or highlight them. Use big print that you can easily see, arrange your notes to fit a set of slides so that you turn a page when you want a new slide. When giving a talk some people use cards they can hold in their hand. All these help you look up and at your audience. You need to see where the chat (if any) is coming from. You need to see faces smile or otherwise respond to what you say for encouragement, or to see if people are listening or if you are on the right wavelength. Be ready to deviate if you see glazed faces, or a different opportunity arises.

Be ready, if necessary, to deviate from the plan. You may have to do this because of an interruption like a fire practice or a pupil being taken ill. If it happens, don't panic. Re-time the activites and make a note on whatever feedback system you have. One of the joys of planning beforehand is that you have thought through the intentions and so know which bits are essential and which can be optional. Sometimes, an interruption can be used; a visitor or a butterfly coming in can become part of the resources.

An example

An adviser shared his Second World War experiences with a group studying that era when making an advisory visit to a class. The teacher requested him to extend his visit to that class to become an added resource. After the lesson the adviser agreed to send in some photographs and other materials about the period to support the work.

Whether it is group work or individual work time, circulate and praise whenever you can, even for just getting on with the task. Try to talk to every member of the class over a few lessons so they all feel watched and valued.

Practical work

Some teachers tend to duck this kind of activity as creating too much work; they fall back on worksheets or straight written activities, as they are cleaner, can be productive and are a lot easier to organise. It is true that active learning with brains engaged can be obtained with such activities, but to reproduce this kind of pupil involvement in their learning gets harder if all the activities are paper based and sedentary. Variety is the key. Some lessons are more physically active than others and clearly, drama and PE are difficult to undertake without pupils leaving their seats, although some 'chalk and talk' sessions are important. Even the great athletes will attend courses and study, and take instruction away from their training and performance sessions. Some subjects are more practically based than others; for example, science and DT require practical work, while the humanities, English and mathematics are usually more sedentary occupations. However, even here, a physically active session will help conceptual understanding particularly in younger children. Fieldwork is essential for geography, but so are activities like model making for understanding river flow or contours. Investigating facsimile documents or interviewing people makes history come alive, as does drama for story and character creation in English. The use of equipment in mathematics is essential ranging from the sand and water of the early years' classes to the compasses and protractors of later mathematics.

Some of the points you need to think about when undertaking practical work are related to working with groups, while others concern the appropriate resources in the right place at the right time. This again is where planning and preparation pay off, including the risk assessment. It may be brief and not written down, but you still need to consider the consequences of planning anything active.

For instance:
Do you have enough and appropriate equipment to prevent disturbances which could be incurred through sharing?
Do all the pupils know how to use the equipment safely? This includes mathematical apparatus like compasses as well as scalpels in science.
Is the equipment itself safe? Are the scissors sharp enough to cut the material you want them used for (blunt scissors even with young children are less safe than sharper ones)?
If it is a demonstration, do the pupils need protective eyewear? Will they all be able to see or might there be some pushing and shoving?
Have you consulted the ASE safety books for primary and secondary science activities (ASE 1996; 2001)?
Have you discussed the risks of lathes or sewing machines or cookers with the relevant teaching staff?
Do you personally have the appropriate footwear for a PE lesson?
Do you know on which occasions protective eyeglasses should be worn?
Do you know where to find the regulations for visits and have you consulted them?

Ending a lesson

Pace the activity/task middle of the lesson sufficiently well so that you give yourself time to draw the lesson to a close. Summing up can be as important as starting the lesson, as it is with those thoughts that the pupils will leave the room. Did the lesson achieve its purpose: 'What did you learn today?' It may be that you want a lengthy time to enable groups to contribute their findings, it may be you just want them to clear up properly, it may even be it will just be a 'complete that for homework'. Whatever happens, dismiss the pupils properly in an orderly way. This means that they will arrive at their next lesson or go home or out to break in a constructive, not destructive, way. Take your time over this; you can let those who are ready or quiet go first, or you can get them to put in their chairs and stand behind them first to calm them. There are various small organisational things that can help this process. Keep an eye out for how different teachers do it, and try the more successful methods, then make the one you like best into a routine.

Reflecting on performance

Jot down quickly any notes for the teacher at the end of your plan or on a post-it or in the communication exercise book and make sure you leave the classroom as you found it – it is not your room. What kind of progress did the pupils make against the learning objective you started out with? [3.2.3]. Then, if you are serious about wanting to reflect on your performance, try out the two following suggestions made for qualified teachers. Pollard (2002: 277) has an interesting model of adult–child interaction; he uses the four-quadrant method and asks teachers to consider where in the diagram a particular practice can be located (see Figure 8.2). It designates one axis on adult involvement, whether high or low,

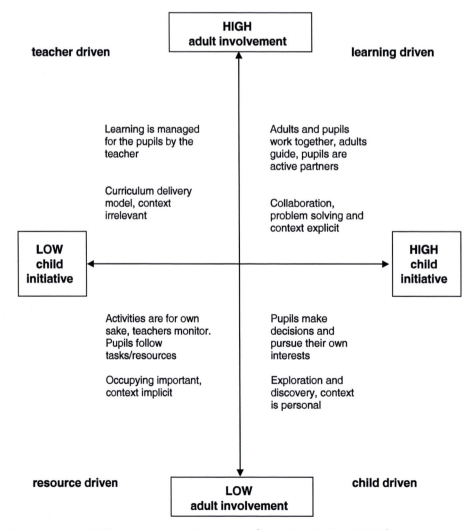

Figure 8.2   Adult–child interaction in classrooms (based on Pollard 2002)

and the other for child initiative, high or low. Where adult involvement is low the activity may be resource driven (low child initiative) or child driven. Where adult involvement is high low child initiative means a teacher-driven lesson. The optimum would be to have a high learning-driven lesson with both high child initiative and maximum teacher involvement. While each lesson should be of a kind fit for its purpose, it does happen that child initiative is more evident in early years' classes, and secondary lessons appear very teacher driven. Pollard suggests that this might be a useful tool when reflecting on the differences between the lesson as it actually took place and what you planned to do.

Another useful self-analysis tool can be found in the *Self-study Materials for Supply Teachers* (DfES 2002a). It looks at three teacher styles, the assertive, the hostile and the non-assertive in terms of the teacher behaviour and the pupil response (see Table 8.1). 'The manner in which you project yourself and respond to pupil behaviour will affect pupils' self-esteem, their attitude to work and their success. Use the following categories to assess your own importance in the classroom. Make notes about how you might improve what you do (DfES 2002a: 107).'

Table 8.1   What style of teacher am I? (from DfES (2002a: 107)

Teacher style	Teacher behaviour	Pupil response
Non-assertive	• Passive • Inconsistent • Reacts to behaviour • Does not plan to manage behaviour • Does not have routines • Does not communicate boundaries to the pupils • Can be led by pupils, e.g. *This is the way we ALWAYS do it*	• Frustration • Tries to manipulate • Escalates situations to find what the 'limits' are • Has no respect for the teacher • Demonstrates anger • Answers back
Hostile	• Aggressive response to pupils • Rigid • Authoritarian • Threatening • Doesn't listen to pupils • Not fair and consistent with all pupils • Expects some pupils to misbehave and often 'labels' them • Confrontational • Sarcastic with pupils	• Fear of making mistakes. Anxious • Low self-esteem • Feels victimised because teacher treats them differently • Feelings of hurt • Doesn't take chances with approach to work • Confrontational
Assertive	• Identifies boundaries • States expectations, both academic and behavioural • Fair and consistent • Listens to pupils • Values pupils' opinions • Good model of behaviour, e.g. polite • Humour – but 'with' children not 'at' them • Praises both achievement and effort	• Understands boundaries • Feels valued • Trusts • Passes opinions • Feels safe and secure • Not frightened of making mistakes • Is more likely to behave positively than negatively

Essential reading

If taking a science lesson:

ASE (1996) *Safeguards in the School Laboratory* (10th edn). Hatfield: Association for Science Education.

ASE (2001) *Be Safe: Health and Safety in Primary School Science and Technology*. Hatfield. Association for Science Education.

Some further reading

DfES (2002a) *Self-study Materials for Supply Teachers: Classroom and Behaviour Management*. London: Department for Education and Skills. (For ideas on the first ten minutes, pp. 78–80; for class management skills, pp. 95, 114–15.)

Elliott, P. (2004a) 'Communication in the classroom', in V. Brooks, I. Abbott and L. Bills (eds) *Preparing to Teach in Secondary Schools*. Maidenhead and New York: Open University Press and McGraw-Hill Education, pp. 96–108.

Hayes, D. (2000) *The Handbook for Newly Qualified Teachers: Meeting the Standards in Primary and Middle Schools*. London: David Fulton Publishers, pp. 73–112.

Hayes, D. (2003) *Planning, Teaching and Class Management in Primary Schools* (2nd edn). London: David Fulton Publishers, pp. 42–86.

Kyriacou, C. (1997) *Effective Teaching in Schools: Theory and Practice* (2nd edn). Cheltenham: Stanley Thornes, pp. 31–63.

Pollard, A. (2002) *Reflective Teaching: Effective and Evidence-informed Professional Practice*. London and New York: Continuum, pp. 259–307.

The Leverhulme Primary Project – classroom skills series:

Brown, G. and Wragg, E. C. (1993) *Questioning*. London and New York: Routledge.

Dunne, E. and Bennett, N. (1994) *Talking and Learning in Groups*. London and New York: Routledge.

Dunne, R. and Wragg, E. (1994) *Effective Teaching*. London and New York: Routledge.

Wragg, E. C. (1994) *Class Management*. London and New York: Routledge.

Wragg, E. C. and Brown, G. (1993) *Explaining*. London and New York: Routledge.

CHAPTER 9

Assessment, monitoring, feedback and recording

The most important thing about teaching is being in the classroom with the pupils; after all, that is where the introduction to learning is taking place. Hopefully, the previous chapters have emphasised how important for the success of that process it is that you understand the learning process itself, provide a supportive learning environment, understand and know subject matter, and plan and prepare. However, there is yet another process to consider if it is true that 'formative assessment . . . is at the heart of effective teaching' (Black and Wiliam 1998: 2). The classroom process is where teacher and learner meet, but it is only part of a continual and complex cycle of activity. A simple diagrammatic version of this was in a previous book (Watkinson 2003) (see Figure 9.1).

What this diagram omits is the effect of the review upon the pupils, who, after all, are the reason for the process in the first place. Teaching and learning are active interfaces of each other. The learning cycle in Chapter 3 needs to be combined with this teaching one.

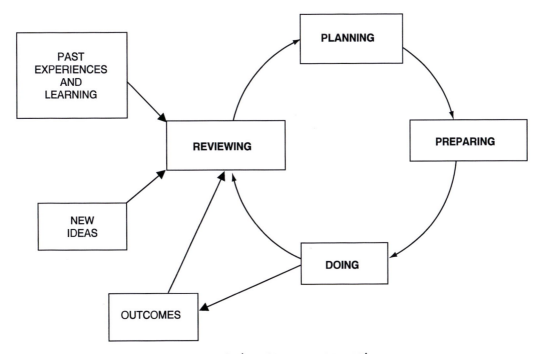

Figure 9.1 The classroom process cycle (Watkinson 2003: 129)

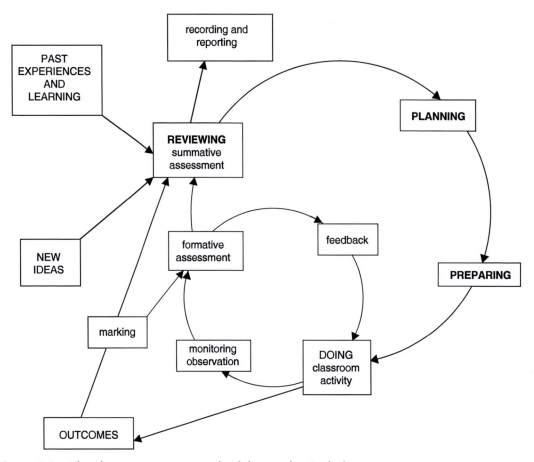

Figure 9.2   The classroom process cycle elaborated to include assessment

Figure 9.2 has some of the various components of assessment and feedback inserted into it. The insertions are in lower case.

Black and Wiliam, who have worked in this field for many years, define assessment as 'all those activities undertaken by teachers, *and by their students in assessing themselves,* which provide information to be used as feedback to modify the teaching and learning activities in which they are engaged' (Black and Wiliam 1998: 2). They found from exhaustive research into the literature that formative assessment effectively raises standards, but that it could be done better, and they found ways of doing it better. It is not just about the teacher understanding the process, but the pupils themselves must use the result of the assessment in order to improve their learning. If the culture is one of 'right answers' only, then pupils assume that if they have not got them, they have failed. But, where the culture is one of success for all, of isolating problems and dealing with them, understanding what is wrong, pupils can improve. 'Opportunities for pupils to express their understanding should be designed into any piece of teaching, for this will initiate the interaction whereby formative assessment aids learning' (ibid.: 11).

Pupils' work can be assessed and monitored as you work together in class, or it can be assessed at the end so that you can see the result of your lesson [3.2.2, 3.3.3]. The final outcome of the lesson may not be seen for many years, as the effect of a teacher or subject being taught may enter the pupils' subconscious only to be recognised in adult life. You only have to read the 'My best teacher' articles in the *TES* to realise the profound and lasting effect some people can have in motivating and empowering individuals. Your main aim will be to monitor work in class to enable the pupils to get the most out of that time. The responsibility for the results of the lesson is the teacher's. Nevertheless, you should discuss the end products, both for your own professional development, to understand the effect you are having on the pupils, and to be able to help pupils achieve even more.

The more you understand the subject matter of the learning objective and the processes of learning itself, the better you will be able to assess whether pupils are doing their best and how you can help them to do better still [3.2.1]. Until you have some criteria to judge progress against you are merely going on hunches and in order to feed back in a meaningful way to the teacher or a pupil you need to know what you are talking about. You will have a lot of experience in judging whether a pupil is working at his or her best in terms of application, effort and so on, but now, as an HLTA, you should begin to see the wider picture of how best to channel that effort, maximise concentration to a purpose and promote interest in further learning. You should be able to grasp what a pupil understands as well as knows and be able to build on that.

But this does not mean you have to be a graduate in a subject to work in such a way [2.1]. 'A high level of subject qualification is less important than a thorough understanding of the fundamental principles of the subject, an understanding of the kinds of difficulties that the pupils might have, and the creativity to think up questions that can stimulate productive thinking' (Black *et al.* 2002: 15). For instance, in mathematics, questioning needs to direct pupils to the different ways to achieve a correct outcome. In science, misconceptions about the world about us can be challenged: does the earth go round the sun or does the sun move during the day from the east to the west? Furthermore, open-ended investigations may have no 'correct' answer. In English, critical appreciation and judgement comes into the assessment process. In understanding the process of learning alongside the subject understanding you will be able to help pupils 'extend their understanding of a concept within a text or to "scaffold" their ideas before writing' (*ibid.*: 17).

Strategies

In assessment you need to recognise what kind of learning outcome is desirable so that you can check for the progress in that area. Are you hoping the pupils are gaining knowledge, a skill, experience or understanding? Is the task practice to get better or to gain new information or to solve a problem? It may be a combination of these, but it shows how vital it is for you to know the teacher's intention.

It does help to think through beforehand not only what the intention of the lesson is, but what success might look like if you achieve it. Some planning formats have a space for success criteria. As with the objectives, it is really helpful to the pupils if they know what success might look like; their idea of success may be to cause the most disruption or get through the lesson not doing anything. Those who finish first may not be the most successful in teacher terms but they think that is what they have to do. Setting achievable targets at the beginning of the task is really helpful, and so you should have some mind-stretchers ready for those who do get there before others.

Verbal

There are various ways to find out what is going on for the pupil apart from formal tests or looking in the records, both of which, however, will help. You can do these with a whole class or individuals. The best way is to ask: get them to tell you! A brainstorming session can be done as a class making webs or lists on the board with key ideas from the pupils, or can be a paper and pencil exercise for a group or individuals. A method used in a large survey on health perceptions with young children was to get pupils to draw pictures of what they know. Concept mapping, where links between ideas are shown, can be in words or pictures. Ask a group or pairs to share what they know with each other before they feed back to the whole class, which can then be developed into a simple game of diamonds where ideas can be ranked, and then the rankings shared with another group. This technique is widely used to teach adults to get them thinking. Open-ended questioning as described in the previous chapter is useful for any sized group.

Examples of verbal assessment, asking really simple questions

It could go like this:
'What are you doing?'
'Colouring in.'
'Why?'
'Because she said so.'
'What for?'
'I don't know.'
'Why this picture?'
'I don't know . . .'

Or it could go like this:
'What are you doing?'
'Drawing this thing.'
'What is it?'
'It is an iron like they used in Victorian times.'
'Why?'
'To see how it is different from my mum's.'
'What is different about it?'
'Well, they didn't have electricity so there isn't a cable . . .'

Can you tell which pupil is learning something from the task they are undertaking? Neither need, adult support to do the task, but both would benefit from adult intervention to enable them to learn more from the task, and your monitoring of either task could improve the situation. The setting of the tasks possibly had the teacher intention of enabling her to help another, small, group, and both may have had a valid curriculum learning objective. The colouring-in could refer to regions on a map, but the simple questions show that the pupil has not grasped the purpose of the exercise, which is something you can soon put right if you monitor through the lesson [3.2.2]. Don't forget to tell the teacher

Photograph 9.1   An HLTA monitoring while responsible for the conduct of the lesson

Photograph 9.2   A TA monitoring with the teacher

if you deviate from the planning for any reason, either responding to the pupils or because of an interruption.

It is also possible that with your style of teaching you encourage pupils to ask questions if they do not understand. The pupil in the first example above could have just asked an adult, 'why have I got to do this?' to have had a much better and more interesting lesson. Instead of getting bored, or bothering their neighbour, they could have completed the task as required and moved on. Just listening to conversations can tell you a lot if you are circulating round a room, even simply whether the pupil is on task. Non-verbal signals such as body posture can tell you a lot about whether the pupil is engaged mentally with the task.

Also, remember that you can give non-verbal feedback through your lack of reply or body language, and a shrug or lack of smile may indicate 'you are wrong' to a pupil, when you actually mean 'yes, but . . .'

Written

It is tempting to rely on the written product of a lesson to show what has been learnt, but the actual act of writing may inhibit some pupils so much that little is committed to paper, leading to a gross underestimate of ability, understanding and knowledge gained. There is still a lot of suspicion about project work done at home, particularly now that the internet is so easily accessible to so many pupils. Can you tell whether the work is that of the pupil or A. N. Other? At least for work done in class you know the input of adult help, and you can observe the amount of joint work going on when monitoring. Make a note of joint working if it was not intended, noting particularly who was sitting next to whom if it is relevant.

Apart from observing and listening to pupils' opinions of what is going on, teachers usually resort to various kinds of testing to try to understand what has been learnt. The trouble with tests is that they only show learning from the test performed, which must always be less than the learning which has taken place. They cannot take account of feelings and attitudes, or the processes which are going on in the pupil's minds, the reasons for lack of understanding or the creative links that might be going on. Investigations into the testing of science some time ago in the old Assessment Performance Unit found that having a picture of a few items could increase the number of correct answers, while actually having real apparatus in front of pupils for them to feel, smell and touch as well as look at would increase the success rate still further. Careful oral questioning with the apparatus could mean even more pupils would succeed. Spelling and tables tests seem straightforward checking devices, but can be used as threats to ensure the words and numbers are learnt elsewhere.

Marking written work must be undertaken only with the direction of the teacher, who must be sure that you understand the criteria to be used. Marking can be destructive, meaningless or helpful according to the methods used; simply writing 'try harder' on a piece of work does not inspire, even if the work is not good enough. Some teachers have told pupils to write the learning objective at the top of the piece of work so that the marking can relate to the objective and offer advice for next steps to be taken. Marks out of ten are relatively meaningless, unless it is clear to both the marker and the pupil what this means. If the marking can include hints for improvement as well as comments on what has been achieved, it can become purposeful.

Marking a set of sums all correct does not necessarily indicate that the pupil is doing well. It might mean the pupil is underachieving and should be further stretched. It is helpful if the culture of the school enables pupils to realise they can learn from their mistakes, and a page with some crosses on shows the learning points. It is particularly helpful if the teacher can see a pattern of mistakes and so can add a remark to point this out to the pupil.

There needs to be a time in the lesson when the marking of previous work can be read and considered by the pupils so that the purpose is achieved. So often books are handed back, or pages stuck in files, all containing comments which have taken the teacher time to write, and they are ignored or not understood by the pupil. Opportunity for the teacher's feedback to be worked on or questioned should be built into the planning.

Using recording sheets

There are various types of recording sheet, the simplest being the mark book, which consists of grids bound in book form similar to a register, where the class lists can be inserted on the left and comments or marks entered on the right. Sharing the marks with the pupils can show them how they are doing.

In the cause of openness some teachers, particularly in KS1, often use graphic designs which can be progressively filled in to show progress; these include walls with bricks to colour in and pictures of animals covered in small boxes. The aim is to share mini-test results such as word lists with the pupils and discuss the progress with them. These should be used with care as the rate of success indicates effectiveness and prolonged use will defeat the object and become demoralising, not helpful.

Using ICT

Recording need not be done in written form by the pupils, so you should not forget the use of cameras, tape and video recorders, all of which older pupils can learn to use and look at for themselves. These are particularly useful for practical work such as DT, for example food technology or textile work, or in the early years where writing is not possible.

Pupil assessment

This can take two forms, one of which is getting the pupils used to self-assessment. Ask:

> What do you think of it?
> Can you read it back to yourself?
> Can you think why you put that?
> Is that your best work?
> Why did you say that?

So that pupils can Black *et al.* (2002) suggest the use of 'traffic light' icons indicate whether they think they have full, partial or little understanding of what has been going on. You can use this as a whole-class strategy with 'hands up' for each category, and then pair up the understanders with the less confident for a discussion session.

Peer assessment can also be useful, but pupils must be trained carefully, as it would be only too easy for a second pupil to tell a first that his or her work is rubbish, and so undo all the good work you and the teacher have been trying to build up in terms of the first pupil's self-esteem; it could even become a form of bullying. So, carefully done by the teacher and built up over time, you could use strategies like getting pupils to read each other's stories and comment, tour round the classroom and look at each others' models or have a discussion of work displayed. 'Pupils came to understand what counted as good work through exemplification'. Peer assessment is not 'just checking for errors or weaknesses. It involves making explicit what is normally implicit, and thus requires the pupil to be active in their learning' (ibid.: 15).

Other types of assessment

The paragraphs above refer to **formative assessment**; it is the most important form although parents, politicians and the media do not always recognise this; it is the most nebulous because it is often not written down. It is informative about learning, enabling teachers and pupils to recognise the extent to which progress is taking place and so act accordingly. It is not easily measurable, and therefore not easily put into a computer, published and compared, even between individual lessons, let alone used for league tables.

The main other type of assessment usually defined is **summative assessment**. This is what takes place at the end of lessons, or a series of lessons, at the end of term or year. The purpose is to sum up what is now known about the subject involved. It is often done in written form, and can thus be marked, frequently in some quantitative form. The resulting numbers can then be manipulated to give aggregates for a group, class or school or even county. This kind of statistical aggregate gives rise to league tables, PANDAs, targets and all the associated angst and fuss that go with them. (PANDAs are Ofsted's annual Performance and Assessment comparison tables which schools receive showing how their school compares with schools of similar size, background and age range in the whole country.)

Some of these factors are easier to see or measure than others. Tests and examinations tend to test knowledge and understanding, and practical skills have to be observed in action as well as examination of an end product, and are more usually seen as part of vocational competence assessment; attitudes are really only seen in the way pupils cope with learning as it happens. Standards have to be established and then monitored in order that results from one teacher or class or school are comparable with those from other places. Individual observers will differ, being different human beings, and so their observations will be subjective. Tests, with limited aims, can be repeated by different people with similar results; the more people who use them and check them the more reliable the results. However, there is always the question of whether a particular test is the valid one to assess a particular area of learning.

Summative assessment usually consists of some kind of test, essay or examination which has been set bearing in mind some national standard, now usually related to the NC. Some of these types of assessment can and should be used for formative assessment, but are not always used like this for various reasons; for example, if the pupil moves on to another class or school, the receiving teacher or organisation often does not have the time to use the results sent to them in any diagnostic way. It can, even may, happen that the receiving organisation distrusts the circumstances under which the tests were done, or didn't like the test used, feeling they know better. However, this kind of assessment is the one used for publication and the results tend to get set in stone, becoming a label for the pupils. Summative test results often end up with pupils being allocated to a particular set or class or even school, thus confining their aspirations or interests to what happens in that place and even moving between groups in an individual class is difficult enough.

Summative assessment is necessary and important, but it is equally important to recognise exactly what is being tested and what can be learnt from the results. A teacher's mark book, with each piece of class or homework marked out of ten according to some criterion known only to the teacher, is useful to that teacher. It usually ranks the members of the class according to their achievement of learning objectives. So, back to the planning and the importance of knowing the learning objective, and the vital need for the pupils to know what the criteria used were and what the objective was, so that they can gain the appropriate marks. If the work is being marked for content, while handwriting and spelling are unimportant for that piece of work, it makes quite a difference to the sort of application the pupil puts into the work. If you are taking over the class and the teacher is marking the work, you need to know what criteria he or she will use in order to aid the pupils to do their best on that occasion. This kind of assessment is called **criterion-referenced**.

National tests are more usually **norm-referenced**. While the teacher may use his or her opinion of what is normal in the class to award marks, where thousands of pupils enter for a test the 'norm' for an age group can be established. Reading tests and NFER (National Foundation for Educational Research) tests brought in by schools for testing verbal reasoning or various subjects have all been norm-referenced with large groups of pupils. Hence teachers have an indication of whether a pupil is performing above or below an average for his or her age against a large sample. NC tests (SATs) and GCSE examinations are criterion-referenced, while grades for exams such as 'A' levels are supposed to be criterion-referenced, which is why increasing numbers of pupils attain the various levels; the levels are not adjusted for the sample, but for the objective of the test.

Kyriacou (1998: 104–5) also describes some other varieties of assessment. While summative assessment is usually used for judging a pupil's progress in educational terms, **diagnostic assessment and testing** is usually performed with a specific objective in view, often more medically or problem based. In schools it is usually done with pupils who are experiencing difficulties, first to diagnose the problem and second to aim for some kind of remedial work. Assessment can be seen as **internal** to the school or **external** as with examinations set by national bodies or examination boards. External assessment can take place within the school, marked by teachers, but it will be moderated and reported externally. **Informal assessment** is that which takes place daily, part of normal classroom practice, and **formal assessment** is usually prepared for and recorded on paper. Assessment can also be **continual** or **terminal** depending on whether the assessment takes place during or at the end of a programme of work performed over a period of time. It can be **objective** as in multiple choice questioning, where there is only one agreed answer, or

subjective as in judging a piece of artwork or writing. Judgement can be made on the **process**, how the activity is carried out, or the end **product**. Most examinations and tests are product based and much of the disagreement about their value is about the need to look at the process by which the product was obtained as well. This is particularly true in science where investigative work is so difficult to examine from the product.

Any kind of test procedure needs careful handling, whether it is an informal observation for interest or a formal external examination. You need to minimise the disruption to normal school life, yet ensure quiet and freedom from interruptions, as even simple assessments like hearing pupils read in the Infants can achieve better results in a calm, friendly atmosphere. Most teachers will welcome questions and suggestions you have about procedures to get the best from pupils, provided you offer them in the usual spirit of constructive support. Some families and cultures are particularly keen on examinations, which will create tension in the home, and many schools now practise for external tests, sometimes to the detriment of covering the curriculum in other areas. The tension can be counterproductive. As well as ensuring the pupils do their best in any kind of assessment or test you must always remember that you have to operate within the framework of the school policies and under the guidance of the teachers. Confidentiality about the process and the results is really important.

When you are discussing the results of testing with the teacher, as you should if you are involved in the planning and feedback of classroom work, ask about the nature of the testing and assessing being done to measure the progress of the pupils so that you are clearer in your own mind about what is really going on [3.2.1]. This should help you interpret what is needed when you take those pupils for extra work, or do some whole-class teaching.

The formative use of summative tests

Much work over the last few years has gone in to trying to make more meaning from summative results by looking at a 'value-added' component. Now it is so easy to put numerical data onto a computer, and all schools have access to some sophisticated software packages, summaries of achievements at various ages are now collated. Entry profiles and baselines are attempted. They seem fairer superficially, but it is difficult to compare understandings of a 5-year-old with the reading ability of a 7-year-old with the literacy level of an 11-year-old with the comprehensive English language qualities of GCSE. However, carefully used, each set of tests can be assessed against the last, and progress or lack of it can be seen, analyses of problems undertaken and targets set.

Test results can be shared with older pupils, and the mistakes explored. If there is a common mistake, it can be used as a teaching point; if there are individual problems these should be explored by the class teacher sensitively and constructively. With younger children, peer marking of tests and an openness about the purpose and nature of the test is still helpful. Careful examination of the end of year optional and national tests at question level can often show up which areas need support in future; for instance, in mathematics, if several pupils find the area questions difficult, so leave them out or answer incorrectly, you know that this needs some work. If their answers given on science papers indicate some common misconceptions, you will have clearer insight into priorities.

Take a weekly spelling test
Each group takes home 20 words to learn each Friday afternoon and there is a class test every Friday morning. Sometimes John gets them all right and other times not.

Talk with the class teacher
Should the individual be put down a group?
Should the teacher or TA spend time with John to ask why there is a difference in performance on some occasions?
Can the teacher or TA see a pattern of difficulty that could be addressed?
Are the lists for learning related to the class's experience?
Are the lists related to each other?
Are the lists just from some book or file which is said to be right for that age?
Are the spellings subsequently used in class work?
How does John feel when he gets things right or gets thing wrong?
Is that important?
Should pupils and parents know the nature of the tests being used?
Why?
Should they know the results of all the tests done in schools?

Black *et al.* suggest that

- Pupils should be engaged in a reflective review of the work they have done to enable them to plan their revision effectively.

- Pupils should be encouraged to set questions and mark answers to help them, both to understand the assessment process and to focus further efforts for improvement.

- Pupils should be encouraged through peer and self assessment to apply criteria to help them understand how their work might be improved.

(Black *et al.* 2002: 14)

Using data and targets

The Primary Strategy guidance (DfES 2004c: 75–9) has a chapter on the use of summative data for formative purposes. At a school level, the data could be used to discuss the pros and cons of setting, whether there are gender differences, whether children coming into the school later than the early years class are getting a helpful start, or whether children of a differing ethnic origin are making appropriate progress. Individual teachers can examine the progress through the year in areas like reading: are those who were two years behind their chronological age at the beginning of the year staying in that position despite the extra booster session, and if so why?

Targets for the end of a key stage in the later years have sometimes been set by outside agencies, regardless of the background or experience of the pupils. It makes more sense to look at a cohort and set a high but attainable target for that year group, considering the needs of the pupils within the cohort. As an HLTA you may be asked not only to input data for analysis but also to participate in the subsequent discussion 'if those are the results what are we going to do about it?' The Primary Strategy guidance (ibid.) suggests 'layering curricular targets', having whole-school targets, broken down into class targets, the differentiated into group targets, and personalised for individual needs where they differ.

Holistic assessment

The Primary Strategy guidance has some useful pages showing how assessment inter-weaves through a lesson as well as being part of the planning, preparation and review cycle. It permeates all that the teacher does (ibid.: 46–9). Looking at the above list of differing assessment methods it is clear that all have a place and, while they look contrasting, a mixture of all the different methods is what is really needed, with a eye on what the purpose of assessing is in the first place. Some of the examples above show how closely linked recording, feedback and assessment are, and how they need to be used together to get the best from all of them; if none is influencing learning they are a waste of time.

A brief note of warning about assessment. Remember, pupils learn at different rates and in different ways, and some of the quiet ones may be bored, some may not understand, others may be thinking things through, and others are just not bothering to do anything. Only when you know the pupils really well can you be sure what is going on. Also, as you are not in charge of the class, you must work to an extent within the strategies normally used within that class. If none of the above kinds of formative assessment is usual in a class you have to take, then just try out one strategy at a time so that the pupils get used to your methods, and discuss what you are doing with the class teacher. 'Mutual observation and the sharing of ideas and experiences about the progress of action plans can give help and support both with the specific techniques and at a strategic level' (Black *et al.* 2002: 23). You may feel you want to take more time to allow for thinking, or spend some time with discussion and questions, for instance. Negotiate that time in your planning sessions if the teacher's demands seem not to allow for this. Strategies like those mentioned above do not have quick results, but sustained work to provide a learning culture rather than a teacher dominated one pays off.

A word of warning from the report *All Our Futures*: The

> multifaceted nature of intelligences has two important implications for education and for creative education in particular. First it is neither accurate nor responsible to judge children's intelligence on the basis of academic ability alone. All the children have a profile of abilities across a wide range of intelligences. Second, children who perform poorly in conventional academic tests may have strong abilities in other areas. Judging children against a single standard of ability can misrepresent their own individual strengths.
>
> (NACCCE 2000: 4)

> As learning is so difficult to see and assess in process, the emphasis has been put on the outcomes of learning – the result of assignments, tests and examinations. We count the number of right answers to our questions and believe this relates to how much the pupil knows … Unfortunately, this emphasis on outcomes has resulted in publicity and even rewards. People move to live in houses in the catchment areas of schools with high places in the league tables, resulting in

more pupils going to those schools, thus more funding. Within schools it has resulted in a disproportionate amount of time in some classes in some schools being spent on revision and rote fact learning and inappropriate booster classes. There are good things to come out of the publicity. It has increased the debate about the purpose of education, it has made some so called 'coasting schools' recognise that their pupils could do better, and some inner city schools realise that other similar schools do enable their pupils to achieve higher standards. Do talk with your mentor or class teacher about their feelings about these matters, recognising the very real tensions that all schools and teachers are under.

(Watkinson 2003: 68)

Record keeping and reporting

Record keeping is an essential for teachers, departments and schools and is not just about pupils' progress but also about changes in the systems and resources used. However, it is in the analysis and use of these records that their usefulness lies. Reporting to parents and carers, to receiving schools or establishments is a must and should be as comprehensive and informative as possible, yet as concise and useful as possible. If progress is tracked through the records, any changes and deviations should be spotted and addressed, and so planning should be done on the basis of recorded progress. Decisions as to future strategies and provision should be made on the basis of what has worked and what hasn't. Records carefully kept during the year can be referred to when compiling reports or doing the 'teacher assessments' which are required as part of the SATs procedures. While records are becoming increasingly open to the person whom they are about, they are not open to just anyone and care should be taken at all times if you are asked to deal with any kind of school records.

When you make any notes, ensure they are accurate, concise, legible and dated and are kept in a secure place, even if you have shared them with the pupils concerned. All the notes should be treated as confidential and either given to the teacher or kept appropriately, and do not forget to anonymise any data you use on a course or assessment. In the unlikely event of your not having any formal planning sheet, just note down anything significant you have observed on a post-it or memo pad; this will help you remember what you want to say when talking to the teacher. This feedback to the teacher may only be informal, but it should be done; for example, if you are working together in the class it may occur just as you leave the room or go for a coffee together. You must maintain a dialogue, because the teacher is responsible for what happens in the classroom [3.2.3].

You may be asked to complete more formal assessment sheets, IEPs or other record sheets as part of your job. If so, ensure you get full instructions about what is required, and be brief, concise and accurate. If possible, get the document typed, but only by a member of the school staff, and always date any such record and sign it. There will be comprehensive policies and guidance about record keeping in your school, so get a copy and ensure you follow what is stated there. There are all sorts of formal records kept in a school, including some medical ones for certain pupils, and your school may keep records of achievement in addition to test results and copies of reports to parents. Teachers may keep portfolios of pupils' work, particularly in subjects like art.

As an HLTA you are more likely than an ordinary TA to be asked to report directly to people other than the teacher, to parent or advisory agencies, for instance, but do remember to consult the class teacher first as he or she is responsible for the teaching and learning and thus for what you say.

It is most unlikely that you will have to complete any formal report on a pupil as this would have to be signed, with your taking responsibility for the content, and that is not your role. Some consideration must also be given to what is shared with parents and carers, and when and where. You may now be involved in supporting a teacher on such occasions, helping at workshop evenings or even in class when parents are invited to see how things actually work in school. Be sure that you are clear of your role on such occasions.

Essential reading

Black, P., Harrison, C., Lee, C., Marshall, B. and Wiliam, D. (2002) *Working Inside the Black Box*. London: nferNelson with King's College London.

Black, P. and Wiliam, D. (1998) *Inside the Black Box*. London: nferNelson with King's College London.

DfES (2004c) *Planning and Assessment for Learning: Designing Opportunities for Learning*. London: Department for Education and Skills.

Some further reading

Brooks, V. (2004) 'Using assessment for formative purposes', in V. Brooks, I. Abbott and L. Bills (eds) *Preparing to Teach in Secondary Schools*. Maidenhead and New York: Open University Press and McGraw-Hill Education, pp. 109–22.

DfES (2002) *Classroom and Behaviour Management*. London: Department for Education and Skills, pp. 67–71.

Kyriacou, C. (1998) *Essential Teaching Skills* (2nd edn). Cheltenham: Nelson Thornes Ltd.

Watkinson, A. (2003b) *The Essential Guide for Experienced Teaching Assistants: Meeting the National Occupational Standards at Level 3*. London: David Fulton Publishers.

CHAPTER 10

In conclusion

Reflective practice

The first book in this pair discussed the importance of your consideration of your job with regard to two factors: first, in terms of your own professional development in improving your skills as an HLTA, particularly observation, and second, in terms of your thinking about your future career. Our ultimate aim in education is to promote learning for all involved, and in schools that means pupils and staff. You may feel, if you have already gained the HLTA status, that you have reached the pinnacle and so do not have to learn any more, that you know all that is needed to do your job.

This is not the case. When dealing with living beings, especially human ones, there are always changes that could be made and new things to learn. In researching for this book, I have found out so many things I wish I had known when a class teacher a head teacher or an adviser. As an adviser I learnt a lot from visiting other schools, so I still make a point of doing this, and find schools still coming up with new ideas, ways and equipment. Sometimes these apparently new things are a return to ways I recognise from 30 years ago, but with different emphases. The reading lists and website lists you will find at the end of the book are one way in which you can extend your views and experiences, but do try to visit other schools, and meet TAs and HLTAs doing things, both different from or similar to you. Most of the books I have suggested you dip into are written for teachers, and an HLTA is not qualified teacher, but the more you understand the teacher's viewpoint the more helpful and knowledgeable you will be. For some of you it is one more step on the way to getting the full training and qualifications. Share your thoughts with the teachers whenever you can and listen carefully to their reasons if they don't agree with what you are saying; they have had so much more training than you have. They will also be a source of useful information and resources. Always keep your critical faculties sharpened so that you can relate new information to your circumstances and values [1.3].

Possibly the most helpful way to look at your practice is with a critical friend, a person who understands the reason for your doing the activity in the first place, who knows you and the circumstances a little, a person who can be positive and see mistakes as things that can be improved rather than things that go wrong. You want somebody to make you feel positive, yet help you move forward. Somebody who just says 'you are doing fine' isn't helpful; you want somebody who works with you as you hope to work with the pupils.

Hopefully; you will be subject to annual performance reviews or appraisals which will offer you just such a chance [1.6].

This book has focused particularly on the theory and practice of what is going on in the classroom in lessons. The new development for HLTAs, as distinct from an experienced TA, is that you are being empowered to take whole classes on an occasional basis in the absence of a teacher, and this is not something you can undertake lightly. As an HLTA you are expected to move the pupils' learning forward but to do this takes not only skill but also an understanding and knowledge of pupils, school policies, the teacher's intentions and the subject matter of the lesson. Most of your time, of course, will still be spent with groups and individuals as part of lessons undertaken by the teachers, but even when you take a class alone, the teachers will be responsible for the outcome. Of course, you will want to do your best in this new situation, so to see how you are doing when taking a whole lesson you can use some of the methods teachers use for self-evaluation.

The really brave get someone to video them and then watch it with a mentor or other critical friend, but that takes both courage and organisation. Also it only reflects one lesson. Hopefully, each lesson is slightly different, responding to the strengths and moods of the pupils and reflecting the nature of the objective. A really powerful way of self-evaluating is to ask the pupils the following (with the agreement of the teacher concerned).

Ask the pupils:
What was the lesson mainly about?
What did you think you were supposed to be learning?
Do you see any connections with other work that you have done in the same subject?
Do you see any connections with work you have done in other subjects?
Did you enjoy the lesson?

(Pollard 2002: 206)

So, you could get into the habit of thinking of different aspects of lessons, or parts of lessons. Hayes (2000: 71) has a list for grading yourself weak/satisfactory/strong/outstanding and there is a useful checklist with key pointers for each element of a lesson on pages 76 and 77 of the supply teacher self-study materials (DfES 2002a). This is set in the form of a table within which you can fill in the empty boxes with notes of ideas to improve certain aspects; Kyriacou has a similar self-appraisal list of typical questions. While they relate to teachers looking at whole lessons, some of the aspects will help you reflect on work with groups and individuals as well.

Just think about one of the following each time you do a lesson and ask yourself:
Did it work for the objective of the lesson?
Could I have done it differently?
What will I do better next time?
Do I need to ask anyone about anything?

Do I need to get any more information about any part of the subject matter or any pupil?
Do I need to tell anyone anything?

- Sufficient and appropriate planning: clear aims
  - breaking down the learning
  - differentiating the learning
  - putting the learning in a context
  - links with past and future intentions of teacher
  - setting targets for learning: individuals, groups or class
  - creating variety
  - new vocabulary to use
  - questions
  - assessment criteria clear

- Preparing the environment for learning
  - resource provision: adequate and suitable
  - room layout
  - equipment set-up properly
  - grouping of pupils

- Lesson introduction: starting points

- Main lesson delivery
  - explanation of task(s): clarity, voice level

- Pupil responses
  - purposefulness
  - level of co-operation
  - interest
  - level of success
  - questioning
  - listening
  - engagement in task
  - attitudes

- My actions
  - questioning
  - listening
  - monitoring
  - feedback including any marking
  - clarity
  - behaviour management strategies used
  - appropriate praise
  - time management

- End part: firm and positive
  - conclusions drawn and future action/scene set

- Relationships with pupils

Kyriacou (1997: 151)

Future prospects for HLTAs

Following the May 2005 General Election, the future of the workforce reform initiative (DfES 2002b) will be one of the topics to be reviewed in the subsequent years. The General Election precipitated the biggest changes for TAs and all support staff since the introduction of SEN funding and locally managed budgets. Adults other than teachers had always been connected to schools in various support categories, but ancillary staff supporting teaching and learning were largely unrecognised as well as untrained. The role of parents as volunteers subsequently increased gradually, largely in primary schools, and money allocated for the support of individual children with special needs was often used to pay for an adult to be in the classroom with the specified pupil. As heads realised the usefulness of this assistance, and with the power and flexibility to employ staff as they felt right, assistants were used in a more general role, and the pupils with special needs became more integrated and included into school life. Delegated budgets started in the late 1980s and early 1990s and it was during the 1990s that the increasing role of TAs became less hidden and, in 1997, recognised in a crucial Green Paper (DfEE 1998). This was the beginning of national induction training, nationally recognised qualifications with the development of national standards, and the beginnings of career pathways.

The workforce remodelling programme brought in the concept of HLTAs, clearly structured, levelled and with nationally agreed task descriptions (NJC 2003), which included the recognition of experience with nationally recognised standards and assessment of status. TA foundation degrees are also now in place and the first graduates are emerging. Some TAs have gone on to become teachers after starting as volunteers, working as TAs, and gaining their degrees and QTS. Ostensibly all the pieces are in place for a fully recognised, trained, tiered workforce of TAs to support teaching and learning. However, this programme has several drawbacks for the government to tackle. This is discussed in the following pages. It's not part of achieving HLTA status but may be of interest if you feel strongly enough to voice your feelings about how the future should be shaped. After all, TAs still do not have a national organisation speaking just for them, or even many local ones.

Pay and conditions of service

There is no nationally recognised pay scale to go with the agreed task descriptions, and even if there were, it is still up to school management to pay whatever they want and whatever they can get staff to work for. The basic scale is less than that of a shelf stacker in a supermarket, but the work is far more satisfying and perhaps convenient for people raising a family. There is no security of tenure other than the general employment legislation available for any part-time worker, so TA and HLTA jobs will be ranked alongside many other similar support staff as flexible employees to be 'hired or fired' according to budget dictates. Gaining HLTA status will not mean an automatic increase in pay rate, which is right, as one should be paid according to the job done, not the qualification. If I worked as a TA, although I am a qualified teacher and have a PhD, I should not expect to be paid any differently from other TAs on the staff; qualifications may be required as a condition of employment, but they do not give rights to certain pay levels.

The aims of the Workforce Remodelling use of HLTAs have been widely debated, and it can be seen as the final piece in the TA jigsaw, a recognition at last of their capability and competence, but for some it has been a step too far. Some teachers feel that under no conditions should anyone other than a qualified teacher be allowed to stand in front of a class, but this argument has been going on since the teacher unions made a similar fuss in the 1960s about anybody other than a teacher being in the classroom at all, when they objected vociferously against ancillary support (NAS 1967; NUT 1962). The introduction of the Specialist Teacher Assistant (STA) award was greeted with cries of 'Mum's Army', and now any kind of assistance is seen as potentially doing teachers out of a job, because they will be 'teachers on the cheap', 'entering teaching by the back door'. This argument actually voices real fears for people who have given many years and much effort to gaining recognition and adequate remuneration as qualified teachers, and personally may have had to make sacrifices in order to gain the qualifications necessary, and it is very interesting to talk to individual teachers across the country about this. On the whole, the usefulness of properly trained assistants is not in dispute, although there are still a few schools which do not have any assistants working in classrooms other than for very specific SEN. There is still a problem for some about Standard 3.3.5c: taking a whole class, yet generally the problem is different, TAs and HLTAs are taking whole classes happily and satisfactorily. The senior management and class teachers alike are saying that they find the TA, who is known to the pupils and who knows the pupils, the ways of the school, the policies and planning strategies, is far more effective with a class in the absence of the teacher than a supply teacher and, they add, 'costs less'. Many aspiring HLTAs, and those who have acquired the status, appear to be paid any higher rate only when they take a class, as a supply teacher would, although a supply teacher day rate includes planning, preparation and marking time. This hourly rate for standing in front of a class was not the intention of HLTA status.

HLTA status is a holistic thing, and I have deliberately cross-referenced the standards as I have gone through the two books, and emphasise again that you need to have all the standards to aspire to the status. The assessment process is also holistic, and not set out like the NVQs can be. You cannot fill in a grid giving evidence for each standard until you have completed the four task formats, showing how you evidence the standards in real situations. Employment at level 4, that anticipated for one who is recognised as an HLTA on the staff, is a whole job, not a 'do it one period and revert to being an ordinary TA' the next; however, you may work most of the day supporting a teacher in the classroom and only take whole classes on your own for PPA time or if a teacher is absent. Standard 3.3.5 covers working with individuals, groups and whole classes, but the NJC description and the national standards taken as a whole cover so much more. If you are planning, preparing, assessing and recording; have the understanding of a specialist area; understand the nuances of teaching and learning as detailed in this book; can lead other adults; work with colleagues and parents; and are still prepared for continuing professional development (CPD), you are working at a higher level all the time. The HLTA role should be seen as similar to a ward or theatre sister in a hospital or a nurse practitioner in a general practice; it is a position in which you should be seen as a senior member of the support staff.

The following job profile (NJC 2003) is so comprehensive it needs adjusting for each individual circumstance, but it clearly indicates a whole job, not a 'take it or leave it' option for part of the day.

Teaching assistant – supporting and delivering learning
Level 4 – To complement the professional work of teachers by taking responsibility for agreed learning activities under an agreed system of supervision. This may involve planning, preparing and delivering learning activities for individuals/groups or short-term for whole classes and monitoring pupils and assessing, recording and reporting on pupils' achievement, progress and development. Responsible for the management and development of a specialist area within the school and/or management of other teaching assistants including allocation and monitoring of work, appraisal and training.

Support for pupils
- assess the needs of pupils and use detailed knowledge and specialist skills to support pupils' learning
- establish productive working relationships with pupils, acting as a role model and setting high expectations
- develop and implement IEPs
- promote the inclusion and acceptance of all pupils within the classroom
- support pupils consistently whilst recognising and responding to their individual needs
- encourage pupils to interact and work co-operatively with others and engage all pupils in activities
- promote independence and employ strategies to recognise and reward achievement of self-reliance
- provide feedback to pupils in relation to progress and achievement

Support for the teacher
- organise and manage appropriate learning environment and resources
- within an agreed system of supervision, plan challenging teaching and learning objectives to evaluate and adjust lessons/work plans as appropriate
- monitor and evaluate pupil responses to learning activities through a range of assessment and monitoring strategies against pre-determined learning objectives
- record objective and accurate feedback and reports as required on pupil achievement, progress and other matters, ensuring the availability of appropriate evidence
- record progress and achievement in lessons/activities systematically and provide evidence of range and level of progress and attainment
- work within an established discipline policy to anticipate and manage behaviour constructively, promoting self control and independence
- supporting the role of parents in pupils' learning and contribute to/lead meetings with parents to provide constructive feedback on pupil progress/achievement etc.
- administer and assess/mark tests and invigilate exams/tests
- production of lesson plans, worksheet, plans etc.

Support for the curriculum

- deliver learning activities to pupils within agreed system of supervision, adjusting activities according to pupil responses/needs
- deliver local and national learning strategies e.g. literacy, numeracy, KS3, early years, and make effective use of opportunities provided by other learning activities to support the development of pupils' skills
- use ICT effectively to support learning activities and develop pupils' competence and independence in its use
- select and prepare resources necessary to lead learning activities, taking account of pupils' interests and language and cultural backgrounds
- advise on appropriate deployment and use of specialist aid/resources/equipment

Support for the school

- comply with and assist with the development of policies and procedures relating to child protection, health, safety and security, confidentiality and data protection, reporting concerns to an appropriate person
- be aware of and support difference and ensure all pupils have equal access to opportunities to learn and develop
- contribute to the overall ethos/work/aims of the school
- establish constructive relationships and communicate with other agencies/ professionals, in liaison with the teacher, to support achievement and progress of pupils
- take the initiative as appropriate to develop appropriate multi-agency approaches to supporting pupils
- recognise own strengths and areas of specialist expertise and use these to lead, advise and support others
- deliver out of school learning activities within guidelines established by the school
- contribute to the identification and execution of appropriate out of school learning activities which consolidate and extend work carried out in class

Line management responsibilities where appropriate

- manage other teaching assistants
- liaise between managers/teaching staff and teaching assistants
- hold regular team meetings with managed staff
- represent teaching assistants at teaching staff/management/other appropriate meetings
- undertake recruitment/induction/appraisal/training/mentoring for other teaching assistants

Experience

- experience working with children of relevant age in a learning environment

Qualifications/training

- meet Higher Level Teaching Assistant standards or equivalent qualification or experience
- excellent numeracy/literacy skills equivalent to NVQ Level 2 in English and Maths
- training in relevant learning strategies, e.g. literacy
- specialist skills/training in curriculum or learning, e.g. bi-lingual, sign languages, ICT

Knowledge/skills
- can use ICT effectively to support learning
- full working knowledge of relevant polices/codes of practice/legislation
- working knowledge and experience of implementing national/foundation stage curriculum and other relevant learning programmes/strategies
- good understanding of child development and learning processes
- understanding of statutory frameworks relating to teaching
- ability to organise, lead and motivate a team
- constantly improve own practice/knowledge through self-evaluation and learning from others
- ability to relate well to children and adults
- work constructively as part of a team, understanding classroom roles and responsibilities and your own position within these

(NJC 2003: 13–15)

You can see that the wording of this job description is similar to but narrower than the job profile given in the NJC guidance.

POSTHOLDER'S JOB PROFILE 2005

Name

Title of Post:	HLTA LEVEL 2
Grade:	Band 4 mid point restricted
Responsible to:	An assigned teacher

Purpose of Job
Provide learning activities for classes under the professional direction and supervision of a qualified teacher. Level 2 HLTAs will plan, prepare and deliver lessons and assess, record and report on development, progress and attainment.

<u>Example duties and responsibilities</u>

SUPPORT FOR TEACHERS
- Organise and manage appropriate learning environment
- Use teaching and learning objectives to plan challenging teaching and learning objectives and to evaluate and adjust lessons/work plans as appropriate within agreed systems of supervision
- Monitor and evaluate pupil responses to learning activities through a range of assessment and monitoring strategies against pre-determined learning objectives
- Provide objective and accurate feedback and reports as required on pupil achievement, progress and other matters, ensuring the availability of appropriate evidence

- Be responsible for recording progress and achievement in lessons/activities systematically and providing evidence of range and level of progress and attainment
- Establish a clear framework for discipline in line with established policy; anticipate and manage behaviour constructively, promoting self-control and independence
- Support the role of parents in pupils' learning and contribute to/lead meetings with parents to provide constructive feedback on pupil progress/achievement etc.

SUPPORT FOR PUPILS
- Supervise pupils engaged in learning activities
- Assess the needs of pupils and use detailed knowledge and specialist skills to support pupils' learning
- Establish productive working relationships with pupils, acting as a role model and setting high expectations
- Promote the inclusion and acceptance of all pupils within the classroom
- Support pupils consistently whilst recognising and responding to their individual needs
- Encourage pupils to interact and work co-operatively with others and engage all pupils in activities
- Promote independence and employ strategies to recognise and reward achievement of self-reliance
- Provide feedback to pupils

SUPPORT FOR THE CURRICULUM
- Deliver learning activities to pupils, adjusting activities according to pupil responses/needs
- Use ICT effectively to support learning activities and develop pupils' competence and independence in its use
- Select and prepare resources necessary to lead learning activities, taking account of pupils' interests and language and cultural backgrounds

SUPPORT FOR THE SCHOOL
- Comply with and assist with the development of policies and procedures relating to child protection, equal opportunities, health, safety and security, confidentiality and data protection, reporting concerns to an appropriate person
- Be aware of and support difference and ensure all pupils have equal access to opportunities to learn and develop
- Contribute to the overall ethos/work/aims of the school
- Establish constructive relationships and communicate with other agencies/professionals, in liaison with the teacher, to support achievement and progress of pupils

PERSON SPECIFICATION
HLTA LEVEL 2

Experience	● Successful recent experience working with children of relevant age in a learning environment
Qualifications/Training	● Meet Higher Level Teaching Assistant standards ● Excellent numeracy/literacy skills – equivalent to at least NVQ Level 2 in English & Maths
Knowledge/Skills	● Can use ICT effectively to support learning ● Full working knowledge of relevant policies/codes of practice/legislation ● Good working knowledge and experience of implementing relevant curricula and other relevant learning programmes ● Good understanding of child development and learning processes ● Good understanding of statutory frameworks relating to teaching ● Constantly improving own practice/knowledge through self-evaluation and learning from others ● Ability to relate well to children and adults ● Understanding classroom roles and responsibilities and your own position within these ● Ability to apply a range of behaviour management policies and strategies which contribute to a purposeful learning environment
Aptitudes	● Work effectively as part of a team and contribute to group thinking, planning etc. ● Effective time management ● Build rapport with adults and children ● To be flexible ● Use own initiative and work independently ● Excellent communication skills with adults and children, verbally and in writing ● Motivate, inspire and have high expectations of pupils ● Creative approach to problem solving ● Ability to adapt quickly and effectively to changing circumstances/situations ● Work calmly under pressure ● Committed to personal and professional development ● Ability to critically evaluate own performance ● Awareness of, and commitment to, equalities issues ● Ability to record and assess pupil progress/performance etc.

....Signed   Date:.................

....   Line Manager

....   Principal

Developments

There will very naturally be developments in the way HLTAs are used, deployed and managed as a result of renewals of contracts and revision of guidance. The pilot of the first run of HLTA assessments was in the autumn of 2003, and 2004 saw the establishment of providers of training across the country, with funding going to the Local Education Authorities (LEAs) for distribution to selected candidates. Different LEAs defined their own selection criteria and different providers operated in different parts of the country; potential HLTAs have had to choose their provider. The provider contracts run to the end of 2005 for briefing sessions, assessment and longer-term course provision. Links have been made for providers of TA Foundation degrees to enable students to gain HLTA status at the same time.

The moderation process for the assessment has been national and rigorously carried out, which itself has enabled a national review of assessment procedures and interpretation of the standards. Already a new version of the guidance to the standards has been produced and national moderation has ensured adherence to the holistic view of the standards. The longer-term courses developed, to train those of you who do not feel ready for assessment without further training, are running but have yet to be evaluated. All this process has been funded and, like any other government initiative, the funding is pump priming, for a limited period only, so it is early days to see where the HLTA scheme will lead.

In the light of the paragraphs above we would all be wise to 'watch this space' and take every opportunity for understanding of the wider picture. Meanwhile, have confidence in your ability to do the job, and enjoy the pupils and the challenge of education in the twenty-first century; you are at the forefront of a movement to increase the opportunities for pupils and those who work with them.

Conclusion

I want to end with the core principles of teaching and learning from the introductory guide to the Primary Strategy CPD materials, which contain whatever phase you are working in, whatever ability pupils or group of adults you are working with, and whatever size group you are leading. You should always remember, however, that you are working under the direction and guidance of a qualified teacher.

Principles for learning and teaching

Set high expectations and give every learner confidence they can succeed

This includes:

- demonstrating a commitment to every learner's success, making them feel included, valued and secure;
- raising learners' aspirations and the effort they put into learning engaging, where appropriate, the active support of parents or carers.

Establish what learners already know and build on it

This includes:

- setting clear and appropriate learning goals, explaining them, and making every learning experience count;
- creating secure foundations for subsequent learning.

Structure and pace the learning experience to make it challenging and enjoyable

This includes:

- using teaching methods that reflect the material to be learned, matching the maturity of the learners and their learning preferences, and involving high levels of time on task;
- making creative use of the range of learning opportunities available, within and beyond the classroom including ICT.

Inspire learning through a passion for the subject

This includes:

- bringing the subject alive;
- making it relevant to learners' wider goals and concerns.

Make individuals active partners in their learning

This includes:

- building respectful teacher–learner relationships that take learners' views and experience fully into account, as well as data on their performance;
- using assessment for learning to help learners assess their work, reflect on how they learn, and inform subsequent planning and practice.

Develop learning skills and personal qualities

This includes:

- developing the ability to think systematically, manage information, learn from others and help others learn;
- developing confidence, self-discipline and an understanding of the learning process.

(DfES 2004d: 14)

Essential reading

DfES and TTA (2003) *Professional Standards for Higher Level Teaching Assistants*. London: Department for Education and Skills and the Teacher Training Agency.

TTA (2005) *Guidance to the Standards: Meeting the Professional Standards for the Award of Higher Level Teaching Assistants*. London: Teacher Training Agency.

References

Abbott, J. (1996) *The Critical Relationship:* Education reform and learning. 1–3. *Education 2000 News.*

Armstrong, T. (1994) *Multiple Intelligences in the Classroom.* Alexandria, VA: ASCD.

ASE (1996) *Safeguards in the School Laboratory* (10th edn). Hatfield: Association for Science Education.

ASE (2001) *Be Safe: Health and Safety in Primary School Science and Technology.* Hatfield: Association for Science Education.

Black, P., Harrison, C., Lee, C., Marshall, B. and Wiliam, D. (2002) *Working Inside the Black Box.* London: nferNelson with King's College London.

Black, P. and Wiliam, D. (1998) *Inside the Black Box.* London: nferNelson with King's College London.

Bowlby, J. (1965) *Child Care and the Growth of Love* (2nd edn). London; Ringwood, Aus.; and Baltimore, MD: Penguin.

Brooks, V. (2004) 'Learning to teach and learning about teaching', in V. Brooks, I. Abbott and L. Bills (eds) *Preparing to Teach in Secondary Schools.* Maidenhead and New York: Open University Press and McGraw-Hill Education.

Bruce, T. and Meggitt, C. (1996) *Child Care and Education.* London: Hodder and Stoughton.

Bruner, J. S. (1966) *Towards a Theory of Instruction.* Cambridge, MA and London: The Belknap Press of Harvard University Press.

Cohen, L., Manion, L. and Morrison, K. (2004) *A Guide to Teaching Practice* (5th edn). London: RoutledgeFalmer.

De Bono, E. (1971) *Lateral Thinking: A Textbook of Creativity.* London: Ward Lock Educational.

De Bono, E. (1972) *Teach Your Child How to Think.* London: Viking.

DfEE (1998) *Teachers Meeting the Challenge of Change* (Green Paper). London: Department for Education and Employment.

DfEE (2000) *Behaviour Management Module: Induction Training for Teaching Assistants.* London: Department for Education and Employment.

DfEE and QCA (1999a) *The National Curriculum: Handbook for Primary Teachers in England; Key Stages 1 and 2.* London: Department for Education and Employment and Qualifications and Curriculum Authority.

DfEE and QCA (1999b) *The National Curriculum: Handbook for Primary Teachers in England; Key Stages 3 and 4.* London: Department for Education and Employment and Qualifications and Curriculum Authority.

DfES (2001) *Special Educational Needs Code of Practice.* London: Department for Education and Skills.

DfES (2002a) *Self-study Materials for Supply Teachers: Classroom and Behaviour Management.* London: Department for Education and Skills.

DfES (2002b) *Time for Standards: Reforming the School Workforce* (Proposals DfES/0751/2002). London: Department for Education and Skills.

DfES (2002c) *Extending Opportunities: Raising Standards.* London: Department for Education and Skills.

DfES (2003a) *Raising Standards and Tackling Workload.* London: Department for Education and Skills with Workforce Agreement Monitoring Group (WAMG).

DfES (2003b) *The Education (Specified Work and Registration) (England) Regulations 2003.* London: Department for Education and Skills.

DfES (2003c) *Excellence and Enjoyment: A Strategy for Primary Schools* (Advice DfES/0377/2003). London: Department for Education and Skills.

DfES (2004a) *Excellence and Enjoyment: Learning and Teaching in the Primary Years* (CD-ROM). London: Department for Education and Skills.

DfES (2004b) *Creating a Learning Culture: Conditions for Learning.* London: Department for Education and Skills.

DfES (2004c) *Planning and Assessment for Learning: Designing Opportunities for Learning.* London: Department for Education and Skills.

DfES (2004d) *Excellence and Enjoyment: Learning and Teaching in the Primary Years – Introductory Guide: Supporting School Improvement.* London: Department for Education and Skills.

DfES and DH (2005) National Healthy School Status: A Guide for Schools (final version 3.8.05). London: Department for Education and Skills/Department for Health.

DfES and TTA (2003) *Professional Standards for Higher Level Teaching Assistants.* London: Department for Education and Skills and Teacher Training Agency.

Dickson, C. and Wright, J. (1996) *Differentiation: A Practical Handbook of Classroom Strategies.* Birmingham: NCET.

Donaldson, M. (1984) *Children's Minds.* London: Fontana Paperbacks.

Dowling, M. (2004) 'Emotional wellbeing', in L. Miller and J. Devereux (eds) *Supporting Children's Learning in the Early Years.* London: David Fulton Publishers.

Dryden, G. and Vos, J. (1994) *The Learning Revolution.* Aylesbury: Accelerated Learning Systems.

Elliott, P. (2004a) 'Communication in the classroom', in V. Brooks, I. Abbott and L. Bills (eds) *Preparing to Teach in Secondary Schools.* Maidenhead and New York: Open University Press and McGraw-Hill Education.

Elliott, P. (2004b) 'Planning for learning', in V. Brooks, I. Abbott and L. Bills (eds) *Preparing to Teach in Secondary Schools.* Maidenhead and New York: Open University Press and McGraw-Hill Education.

Elton, R. (1989) *Discipline in Schools* (Report of the Committee of Enquiry). London: Department of Education and the Welsh Office.

Fisher, R. (2004) *Metacognition* from DfES *Excellence and Enjoyment: Learning and Teaching in the Primary Years* (CD-ROM). London: Department for Education and Skills.

Fox, G. (1998) *A Handbook for Learning Support Assistants.* London: David Fulton Publishers.

Fox, G. (2001) *Supporting Children with Behaviour Difficulties.* London: David Fulton Publishers.

Goleman, D. (1996) *Emotional Intelligence.* London: Bloomsbury.

Greenfield, S. (2005) 'Answer quick, question poor', *Times Educational Supplement,* 28 January 2005.

Griffin-Beale (ed.) (1979) *Christian Schiller in His Own Words.* London: A & C Black.

Harlen, W., Darwin, S. A. and Murphy, M. (1977a) *Match and Mismatch: Finding Answers.* Edinburgh: Oliver and Boyd for the Schools Council.

Harlen, W., Darwin, S. A. and Murphy, M. (1977b) *Match and Mismatch: Raising Questions.* Edinburgh: Oliver and Boyd for the Schools Council.

Hay/McBer (2000) *Research into Teacher Effectiveness* (Phase II). London: Hay/McBer.

Hayes, D. (2000) *The Handbook for Newly Qualified Teachers: Meeting the Standards in Primary and Middle Schools.* London: David Fulton Publishers.

Hayes, D. (2003) *Planning, Teaching and Class Management in Primary Schools* (2nd edn). London: David Fulton Publishers.

Holt, J. (1964) *How Children Fail.* London: Penguin Books.

Holt, J. (1967) *How Children Learn.* London: Penguin Books.

Hook, P. and Vass, A. (2000) *Creating Winning Classrooms.* London: David Fulton Publishers.

Hughes, P. (2004) 'Learning and teaching: what's your style', in C. Bold (ed.) *Supporting Learning and Teaching.* London: David Fulton Publishers.

Isaacs, S. (1929) *The Nursery Years.* Frome and London: Butler and Tanner Ltd.

Jarvis, P., Holford, J. and Griffin, C. (1998) *The Theory and Practice of Learning.* London: Kogan Page.

Kyriacou, C. (1997) *Effective Teaching in Schools: Theory and Practice* (2nd edn). Cheltenham: Stanley Thornes.

Kyriacou, C. (1998) *Essential Teaching Skills* (2nd edn). Cheltenham: Nelson Thornes Ltd.

Lazear, D. (1994) *Seven Pathways of Learning: Teaching Students and Parents about Multiple Intelligences.* Tucson, AZ: Zephyr Press.

Lee, V. (1990) *Children's Learning in School.* London: Hodder and Stoughton for the Open University.

MacGilchrist, B. and Buttress, M. (2005) *Transforming Learning and Teaching.* London; Thousand Oaks, CA and New Delhi: Paul Chapman Publishing, Sage Publications Inc. and Sage Publications India Pvt Ltd.

MacGilchrist, B., Myers, K. and Reed, J. (1997) *The Intelligent School.* London: Paul Chapman.

MacGilchrist, B., Myers, K. and Reed, J. (2004) *The Intelligent School* (2nd edn). London; Thousand Oaks, CA and New Delhi: Sage.

Marshall, S. (1963) *An Experiment in Education.* Cambridge: Cambridge University Press.

McIntyre, D. (2000) 'The nature of classroom teaching expertise', in D. Whitebread (ed.) *The Psychology of Teaching and Learning in the Primary School*. London and New York: RoutledgeFalmer.

Mortimore, P. (ed.) (1999) *Understanding Pedagogy and Its Impact on Learning*. London; Thousand Oaks, CA and New Delhi: Paul Chapman, Sage Publications Inc. and Sage Publications India Pvt Ltd.

Muijs, D. (2004) 'Understanding how pupils learn: theories of learning and intelligence', in V. Brooks, I. Abbott and L. Bills (eds) *Preparing to Teach in Secondary Schools*. Maidenhead and New York: Open University Press and McGraw-Hill Education.

NACCCE (2000) *All Our Futures: Creativity, Culture and Education* (Report to Secretaries of State for Education and Employment, and Culture Media and Sport). London: Department for Education and Employment: National Advisory Committee on Creative and Cultural Education.

NAS (1967) *Teachers Aides: Helps or Substitutes*. London: National Association of Schoolmasters.

Neill, A. S. (1962) *Summerhill*. London: Victor Gollancz.

NJC (2003) *Support Staff: The Way Forward*. London: Employers' Organisation for the National Joint Council for Local Government Services.

NRT (2004) *Time for Standards: Planning, Preparation and Assessment Strategies – Good Practice* (NRT/0025/2004). London: National Remodelling Team: Department for Education and Skills.

Nuffield Primary Science (1967) *Teachers' Guide*. London: Collins.

NUT (1962) *The NUT View on Ancillaries and Auxiliaries*. London: National Union of Teachers.

Ofsted (1993) *Handbook for the Inspection of Schools*. London: Her Majesty's Stationery Office.

Ofsted (2003) *Handbook for Inspecting Nursery and Primary Schools* (May 2003, Vol. HMI 1359). London: Office for Standards in Education.

Plowden, B. (1967) *Children and Their Primary Schools* (A Report of the Central Advisory Council for Education England, Volume 1). HMSO.

Pollard, A. (2002) *Reflective Teaching: Effective and Evidence-informed Professional Practice*. London and New York: Continuum.

Riding, R. (2002) *School Learning and Cognitive Style*. London: David Fulton Publishers.

Riding, R. and Rayner, S. (1998) *Cognitive Styles and Learning Strategies*. London: David Fulton Publishers.

Rogers, B. (1991) *You Know the Fair Rule*. Harlow: Longman.

Scoffham, S. (2003) *Teaching, Learning and the Brain. Education 3–13*, 31(3), 49–58.

Senge, P. M., Cambron-McCabe, N., Lucas, T., Smith, B., Dutton, J. and Kleiner, A. (2000) *Schools that Learn*. London and Yarmouth, ME: Nicholas Brealey Publishing.

Shayer, M. and Adey, P. (1981) *Towards a Science of Science Teaching: Cognitive Development and Curriculum Demand*. London: Heinemann.

Shayer, M. and Adey, P. (eds) (2002) *Learning Intelligence: Cognitive Acceleration Across the Curriculum from 5 to 15 Years*. Buckingham and Philadelphia: Open University Press.

Smith, A. (1996) *Accelerated Learning in the Classroom*. Stafford: Network Educational Press Ltd.

Stubbs, M. (2003) *Ahead of the Class*. London: John Murray.

Titman, W. (1994) *Special Places, Special People: The Hidden Curriculum of School Grounds*. Godalming: World Wildlife Trust and Learning Through Landscapes.

TTA (2005) *Guidance to the Standards: Meeting the Professional Standards for the Award of Higher Level Teaching Assistants*. London: Teacher Training Agency.

TTA and DfES (2002) *Qualifying to Teach: Professional Standards for Qualified Teacher Status and Requirements for Initial Teacher Training*. London: Teacher Training Agency and Department for Education and Skills.

Watkins, C. and Mortimore, P. (1999) 'Pedagogy: what do we know?', in P. Mortimore (ed.) *Understanding Pedagogy and Its Impact on Learning*. London; Thousand Oaks, CA and New Delhi: Paul Chapman Sage Publications Inc. and Sage Publication India Pvt Ltd.

Watkinson, A. (2002) *Assisting Learning and Supporting Teaching: A Practical Guide for the Teaching Assistant in the Classroom*. London: David Fulton Publishers.

Watkinson, A. (2003a) *The Essential Guide for Competent Teaching Assistants: Meeting the National Occupational Standards at Level 2*. London: David Fulton Publishers.

Watkinson, A. (2003b) *The Essential Guide for Experienced Teaching Assistants: Meeting the National Occupational Standards at Level 3*. London: David Fulton Publishers.

Watkinson, A. (2005) *Professional Values and Practice: The Essential Guide for Higher Level Teaching Assistants*. London: David Fulton Publishers.

Wood, D. (1988) *How Children Think and Learn*. Oxford and Cambridge, MA: Blackwell.

Useful websites

www.acceleratedlearning.com (for accelerated learning skills)

www.curriculumonline.gov.uk (for curriculum support materials)

www.dfes.gov.uk (for the latest educational news and links to other sites)

www.dfes.gov.uk/leagateway (to find your LEA website)

www.fultonpublishers.co.uk (for useful books for TAs, teaching and learning, and SEN specialisms)

www.hlta.gov.uk and www.tta.gov.uk/hlta (for general information about and for HLTAs)

www.lg-employers.gov.uk (for information about national occupational standards and general advice for support staff, job descriptions, pay and conditions, and other support staff information)

www.lsc.gov.uk (for help with English and mathematics qualifications training)

www.nc.uk.net (for curriculum information and support materials for inclusion, SEN and G&T)

www.ncaction.org/creativity (for the government website supporting creative work)

www.ngfl.gov.uk (for general gateway to educational resources)

www.qca.org.uk (for support materials, especially schemes of work and assessment information)

www.remodelling.org (for up-to-date information and details about the workforce remodelling initiative)

www.standards.dfes.gov.uk (for statistics and strategy materials)

www.teach.gov.uk (for help with routes into teaching)

www.teach.gov.uk (for information on training to be a teacher)

www.teachernet.gov.uk (for support materials and documents in general)

www.teachernet.gov.uk/teachingassistants (for general information for TAs)

www.tta.gov.uk/hlta (for general information about and for HLTAs)

www.21learn.org (for the 21st Century Learning Initiative)

Professional associations or unions used by TAs

www.gmb.org.uk – a union for support staff

www.napta.org.uk – an association formed by Pearson Publishing to provide services to TAs www.pat.org.uk – Professionals Allied to Teaching (PAtT): accessible via the Professional Association of Teachers (PAT)

www.unison.org.uk – a union for support staff

The main teachers' associations

www.nasuwt.org.uk (for National Association of School Masters and Union of Women Teachers (NASUWT))

www.teachers.org.uk (for National Association of Teachers (NUT))

www.teacherxpress.com (for Association of Teachers and Lecturers (ATL))

Subject association websites

Design and technology: www.data.org.uk – Design and Technology Association

English: www.nate.org.uk – National Association of Teachers of English

Mathematics: www.m-a.org.uk and www.atm.org.uk – Mathematics Association and Association of Teachers of Mathematics

Science: www.ase.org.uk – Association for Science Education

Also useful is the ICT support website: www.becta.org.uk – British Educational Communications and Technology Agency, a UK agency supporting ICT developments

Index